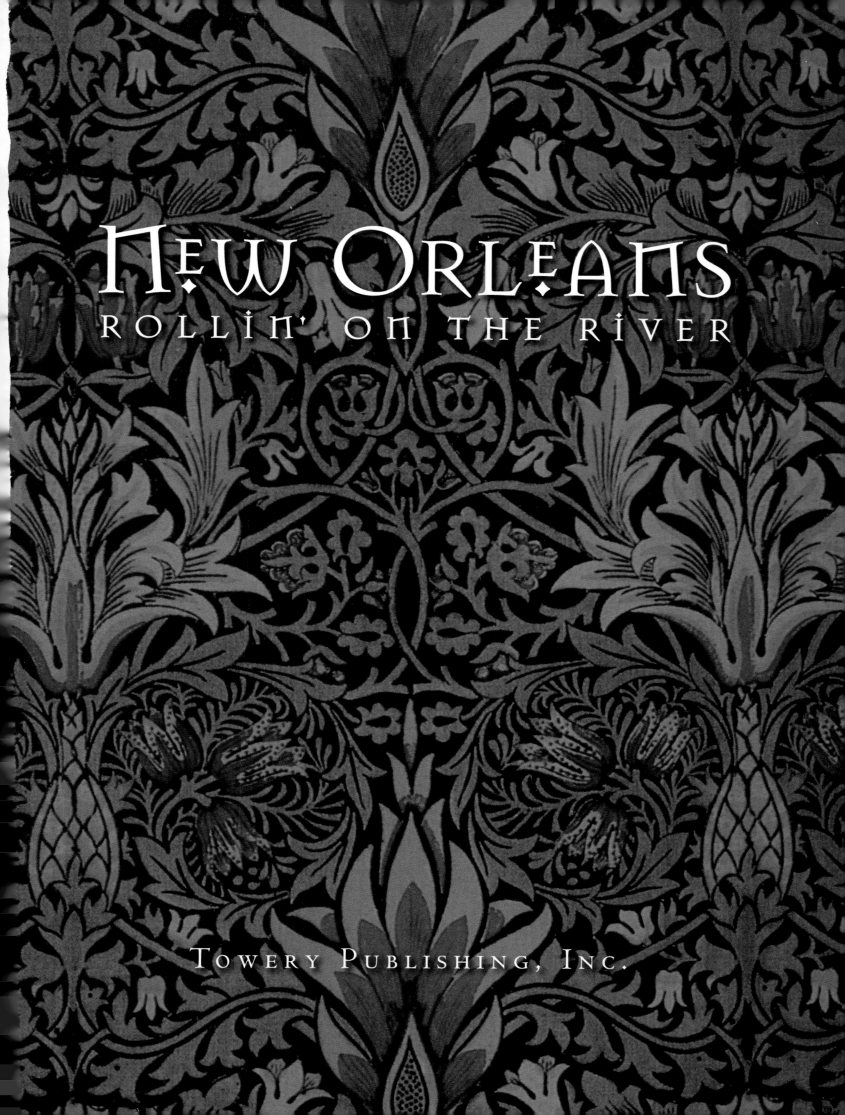

NEW ORLEANS
ROLLIN' ON THE RIVER

TOWERY PUBLISHING, INC.

New Orleans
Rollin' on the River

By Angus Lind

✤

Photography Editing and Captions by
Michael Tisserand

✤

Profiles in Excellence by
Paul F. Stahls Jr.

✤

Art Direction by
Jil Foutch

URBAN
TAPESTRY
SERIES
Towery
PUBLISHING, INC.

LIBRARY OF CONGRESS CATALOGING-IN-PUBLICATION DATA

Lind, Angus, 1944-
  New Orleans : rollin' on the river / by Angus Lind ; photography
editing and captions by Michael Tisserand. Profiles in excellence /
by Paul F. Stahls, Jr.
    p. cm. -- (Urban tapestry series)
    Includes index.
    ISBN 1-881096-36-X (alk. paper)
    1. New Orleans (La.)--Civilization.   2. New Orleans (La.)-
  -Economic conditions.   3. New Orleans (La.)--Pictorial works.
  4. Industries--Louisiana--New Orleans.   I. Tisserand, Michael,
  1963-   . II. Stahls, Paul F.   III. Title.   IV. Series.
  F379.N55L56   1996
  976.3'35--dc20   96-36009
                                                                              CIP

Towery Publishing, Inc., 1835 Union Avenue, Memphis, TN 38104

PUBLISHER: J. Robert Towery
EXECUTIVE PUBLISHER: Jenny McDowell
NATIONAL SALES MANAGER: Stephen Hung
NATIONAL MARKETING DIRECTOR:
  Eleanor D. Carey
MARKETING COORDINATOR:
  Carol Culpepper
PROJECT DIRECTORS: Marilyn Greiner, Jacalyn
  McNamara, Robert Philips
EXECUTIVE EDITOR: David B. Dawson
SENIOR EDITOR: Michael C. James

PROFILES MANAGER/ASSOCIATE EDITOR:
  Mary Jane Adams
ASSOCIATE EDITORS: Lori Bond, Lynn Conlee,
  Carlisle Hacker
ASSISTANT EDITOR: Jennifer Cobb
EDITORIAL CONTRIBUTOR: Michael Fay
PROFILE DESIGNERS: Jennifer Baugher,
  Laurie Lewis, Ann Ward
TECHNICAL DIRECTOR: William H. Towery
PRODUCTION MANAGER: Brenda Pattat
PRODUCTION ASSISTANT: Jeff McDonald

Contents

EEN THERE. DONE THAT. FOR BETTER OR worse, that's pretty much the mind-set of New Orleans when it comes to trying to prove itself. There isn't the citywide energy you find in Atlanta. There isn't the penchant for building newer and bigger buildings as there is in Dallas. People are not so busy making money that they don't have time to enjoy it, like in Houston.

Eternally compared to those three cities, a stylish decadence and a different set of priorities have long saved New Orleans from their fates. We were a transportation leader in the South, shipping via the river and railroads. We've been an international port city forever. We were

In the evening the French Quarter seems to glow from within (LEFT). The majestic St. Louis Cathedral and ubiquitous webs of ironwork provide old-world ambience (OPPOSITE).

once the boxing and horse racing capital of the country, and even though those days have come and gone, the accomplishments are in the history books. We're a grand old city, and we've settled in to enjoy life and let those others duke it out for whatever title they want.

We're also not some nouveau tourist destination discovered by yuppies and marketed by slick travel agent packages and condo developers. We've been doing this tourist thing for ages. It's just that now we're better at it and more focused on it since tourism seems to have

overtaken the port and oil and gas as the city's top industries.

And fortunately, there's just enough vibrancy and progress to ward off two ever-present annoy-ances: apathy, a spin-off of the *joie de vivre* and *laissez les bon temps rouler* mentality that pervades this city; and our infamous politics as usual. But it is a constant battle.

New Orleans is the city where people say "ersters" for oysters and "erl" for oil. It's the only city whose domed stadium looks like the top of a roll-on deodorant, and it's the city that is the birthplace of the take-out daiquiri. (Thought I was going to say jazz, didn't you? Well, it's that too.)

AMONG NEW ORLEANS' MANY vibrant African-American tra-ditions are two that developed during Carnival season: the Mardi Gras Indians (ABOVE) and the Zulu Parade (OPPOSITE).

New Orleans is a city where style and grace are much more impor-tant than speed and pace. More than any other group, New Orleanians worship leisure time with a religious fervor. And under the heading of leisure time fall the subcategories of food, drink, music, and partying. Rest assured, those are the priorities of this city. We are the self-anointed, if not the acknowledged, leader in partying and throwing parties. Accept no substitutes.

Each spring there's the New Orleans Jazz & Heritage Festival, a two-week celebration of—what else?—music, food, and drink at the historic New Orleans Fair Grounds, where only a month before, aspir-ing candidates for the Kentucky Derby tune up in the Louisiana Derby.

Top national and local names in the music world entertain thousands of visitors and natives who soak up the sun; dance; dine on such Louisiana delicacies as andouille sausage, red beans and rice, alligator sauce piquante, crawfish étouffée, and po'boys (our signature sandwich); and wash it all down with beer after beer.

Earlier in the year, there's the Carnival season, a two-week marathon of debauchery where maskers on floats ride through the streets tossing worthless beads and other throws to thousands of onlookers who fight each other for plastic cups, Frisbees, doubloons, and even panties. On Fat Tuesday—the final day in this Carnival season and the day before Lent begins in this very Catholic, very French city—a million-plus people masquerade, stand in the streets, party, and witness hundreds of floats and a few risqué scenes, such as women along the parade route and on French Quarter balconies baring their endowments in exchange for throws. We dub this quiet little gathering Mardi Gras. Perhaps you've heard of it.

But Carnival isn't just floats and krewes, kings and queens, beads and booze. It's a state of mind. And it, too, is a priority.

© MICHAEL P. SMITH, NEW ORLEANS

THERE ARE MORE PARADES HERE, WE'RE CON-vinced, than in any other city in the world. Lent allegedly ushers in the somber season, but a couple of weeks into it, up pop about 30 St. Patrick's Day and St. Joseph's Day parades and gatherings, and if you'd ever witnessed them, you'd understand why "allegedly" is the working word in this sentence. There is also the Italian Open golf tournament, whose symbol is a martini glass, and the French Quarter and Bourbon Street, wide open with no closing times, 365 days a year. There's Pat O'Brien's—and its famed drink, the potent Hurricane—which lurks nearby on St. Peter Street. Pat O's, as the natives who frequent this legend-ary establishment refer to it, has the largest volume of liquor sales in the world. So much for Lent.

Then there's the music. Where do you start? Brass bands. Zydeco. Cajun music. The blues. Jazz. The Neville Brothers. Aaron Neville. Charmaine Neville. Dr. John. Fats Domino. Pete Fountain. Harry Connick Jr. Wynton and Branford Marsalis, or their dad, Ellis. Irma Thomas. Al Hirt. Cowboy Mouth. Frogman Henry. Ernie K-Doe. Louis Armstrong. Jelly Roll Morton. Buddy Bolden.

The city's coroner, Frank Minyard, plays the trumpet. The district

▲ PHILIP GOULD

THERE ARE MANY REASONS AND seasons for wearing green. At Pat O'Brien's more alcohol is served than at any other bar in the world. And on St. Pat's Day, the Irish (and the honorary Irish) strut their stuff in a grand parade in the Irish Chan-nel neighborhood.

▲ PHILIP GOULD

THE NEW ORLEANS JAZZ & Heritage Festival is an annual rite of spring. Among the many Louisiana voices you'll hear at the fest are (CLOCKWISE FROM ABOVE) Aaron Neville's fluttering falsetto, D.L. Menard's Cajun cries, Marva Wright's powerhouse gospel and blues, and Nathan Williams' zydeco squeeze box. Meanwhile, the House of Blues has nightly shows that include both national acts and such notable locals as Walter "Wolfman" Washington (CENTER).

▲ RICHARD PASLEY PHOTOGRAPHY

attorney, who just happens to be Harry Connick Sr., sings in piano bars. Music is everywhere, from the storied and funky Tipitina's nightclub on Tchoupitoulas Street, where Professor Longhair did his piano thing, to Dan Aykroyd and friends' House of Blues in the French Quarter.

Familiar to all New Orleanians are "second liners," the marchers who follow a jazz parade, carrying umbrellas and waving bandannas known as "dew rags." Music and parades are so much a part of our lives that they even follow some of us into death. When one of our famous musicians dies, there is frequently a jazz funeral, complete

with a parade all the way to the cemetery. The band, on the way to the graveside, plays mournful dirges, but after the burial and "dismissal" services, it picks up the beat and the second liners dance to the music. The tempo change is supposed to provide the deceased a happy journey into the great beyond. The same bandannas that were used to dry tears only moments before become celebratory handkerchiefs to be waved. That's where the term dew rag is said to have originated. Curiously, one of the best-named upbeat songs is "I'm Glad You're Dead, You Rascal, You."

▲ PHILIP GOULD

Scores of weekend festivals in and around the New Orleans area honor every crustacean and shellfish known to man, and keep the social calendar rolling virtually year-round. The Chalmette Crawfish Festival. The Lacombe Crabfest. The Bridge City Gumbo Festival. Even the lowly nutria, a swamp rat and a major nuisance because it burrows and undermines canals, has attracted a celebration.

Oh yes, did we mention that New Orleans has hosted more Super Bowls than any other city? We host our eighth in 1997. It's no secret why the National Football League likes to come here for its big

Gourmet meals can be sumptuous or straightforward, tony or decidedly proletariat. Sauce-drenched entrées are the hallmark of traditional Creole cuisine. For lunch, locals wash down boiled (or "berled") crabs and muffulettas with a cold Dixie longneck. Whatever you eat, watch out for the hot peppers; with these on board, some of your food may bite back.

party—and it's *not* for the central location.

But it *could* be for the food. The food . . . well, the food is something else. Always has been. Always will be. Mouthwatering, hot and spicy, intriguing, mystical concoctions. Roux, gumbos, stews, étouffées, and bisques. Oysters, crawfish, crabs, shrimp, redfish, speckled trout, catfish, and alligator. Boiled, broiled, blackened, fried, and smothered in sauces made of herbs and spices found nowhere else. Trout amandine. Trout meunière. Trout marguery. In a city as Catholic as this one, everybody knows what the Holy Trinity is. But in culinary

circles, the hailed trinity consists of onions, celery, and bell peppers. Then there's cayenne pepper, Louisiana hot sauce, and pungent crab boil. Mystifying to some, intimidating to a few, appealing to all—food and restaurants are to New Orleans what the Cubs are to Chicago and Broadway is to New York.

Consequently, the subject of good food, how to cook it, and where to eat it never goes out of season. If you took the restaurants out of New Orleans, it's been said, you might as well change the course of the Mississippi River and let it flow somewhere else. Ella Brennan, of the internationally acclaimed Commander's Palace restaurant in the city's

I F YOU'RE LOOKING FOR A HISTORY lesson, just start eating and drinking. Dating back to 1840, Antoine's is the city's oldest restaurant, where tuxedoed waiters still offer French menus (OPPOSITE). It was 1821 when New Orleans' Napoleon House (LEFT) was offered as a home to the exiled emperor, then languishing in St. Helena. Although Napoleon died before the rescue plot could be carried out, the now-famous bar that bears his name lives on.

historic Garden District, likes to tell this story: "There used to be this girl who worked for us, and she used to say, 'Food in New Orleans is like sex—everybody's interested.' Why is it so popular? Because it has taste. If you go eat in most cities, even in France, the food in New Orleans is better. French techniques are the basis of almost all good cooking, but it's very subtle. New Orleans food hits you over the head and makes you say, 'Wow!' It has taste and aftertaste, and it's not subtle."

One of the most amusing things in such oyster houses as the Acme or Felix's, both in the French Quarter, is to watch tourists attempting

to eat raw oysters for the first time. For some, fear and trepidation do not adequately describe the experience of topping this tasty but slimy gray bivalve mollusk with horseradish, hot sauce, ketchup, and lemon, and then stabbing it with a cocktail fork and putting it into your mouth. Some never manage to get one down. But others thrive on them. At the Acme, the house record is an incredible 27 dozen, set by one Frank Nemic of Cicero, Illinois, in 1988. For the math impaired, that's 324 of those creatures. No count available on how many pearls were found.

Another challenge is learning how to peel and eat boiled crawfish, those succulent diminutive lobsters. How something so tasty could come out of a mud hole in the side of a bayou is truly one of God's miracles. Natives who are adept at demolishing pounds of these crustaceans—which are also known as crawdads and mud bugs—use a technique that sounds disgusting: They suck the heads and pinch the tails. And that's exactly what they do. They split the crawfish in half, suck the head for the spicy crab boil and seasonings the mud bugs are cooked in, and pinch the tail to remove the meat. It's as simple as that. Try it sometime. Nick Stipelcovich, owner of three area bars—the Triangle

West, Gennaro's, and the Lantern Lounge—is the current crawfish-eating champion. At the Breaux Bridge Louisiana Crawfish Festival, he downed more than 55 pounds in 46 minutes. Don't even think about trying that.

A word to the wise: Don't come here to diet. It's impossible. Willpower? What's that? Know the old saying "Bend but don't break"? You'll break. Because there's no other cuisine anywhere in the world like New Orleans Creole and Cajun, and there never will be. And that's partly because of our history and partly because of our geography. You don't know it when you drive or fly in, but New Orleans is really an island town, the only inland island in the United States. We are buffered, cordoned off not only from the rest of the country, but also from the rest of the state. To the north is mammoth Lake Pontchartrain. To the east is Lake Borgne. Big Muddy, the Mississippi River, curls its crescent around us like a serpent. To the south is the Gulf of Mexico, spawning ground for hurricanes. And to the west, bayous and swamps, fraught with alligators and crawfish and populated by the French-speaking Cajuns who came here from Acadia (Nova Scotia) after being expelled by the British in the mid-1700s.

MANY CONSIDER NEW ORLEANIANS' cravings to be a bit strange, but it certainly makes for interesting cuisine. For Louisiana lobster, start with a kettle of bayou crawfish, boiled with seasonings. For New Orleans sushi, visit a local oyster bar and order up a dozen raw ones on the half shell.

EW ORLEANS WAS FOUNDED ALMOST 300 years ago by the French, who may or may not have realized that their new city was surrounded by water and marsh. Situated six feet below sea level, New Orleans was built on a mosquito-infested swamp where no one in his right mind should have built a city. Yet because of this location—at the mouth of the mightiest river in America—we've been able to maintain our heritage and traditions, and

I N EARLY NEW ORLEANS, THE flags of nations were traded back and forth like insults on a playground. This history can be viewed in the flags that now fly over the Omni Royal Orleans hotel and on the historical markers that reveal the various names once held by French Quarter streets.

insulate ourselves from certain aspects of a country whose cities have been homogenized. There wasn't a bridge over any of this water until 1935 and even then it wasn't located in the heart of the city. So because of this port of entry, an unlikely and exotic mix of French, Spanish, English, Irish, Caribbean and African blacks, Germans, Sicilians, Yugo-slavians, and Native Americans settled here. And later Central Americans and Vietnamese would come. Basically, throughout New Orleans' history, everyone has gotten along together pretty well. Historians say

New Orleans was the first city referred to as a melting pot. We learned from each other. Today's food, language, and lifestyle are a product of all these intermingling cultures and cuisines.

Sure, our language can be difficult to understand. Yes, our way of life is different, and yes, because of our watery existence, we bury our dead above ground in tombs, many of which are architectural master-pieces. Our streets, no matter how much maintenance they get (which is, generally speaking, not much), have forever been a monument to

DURING HURRICANE SEASON (June through November), near-daily cloudbursts open over the city, washing the Cabildo on Jackson Square and providing happy relief from summer heat.

potholes because of the boglike subsurface they are built on. The rain doesn't help this situation either. We get almost 60 inches a year. Just think tropical and you'll be fine. And that's why we walk slowly here. You would too, especially in August, when 95 meets 95 (temperature and relative humidity). But we don't talk slowly despite what you might think. And you're about to find out why.

EW ORLEANS IS STEEPED IN LITERATURE. Tennessee Williams wrote *A Streetcar Named Desire* here. Anne Rice of *The Vampire Chronicles* fame lives here. John Grisham's *The Pelican Brief* was set here. But in recent years, while much has been written about New Orleans and while it has become a popular venue for movie-makers and novelists, the nation has also been fed tons of misinformation. Americans have heard that most New Orleanians travel by pirogues through bayous, dodging alligators as they go; that everyone calls each other "cher"; that Cajuns and Creoles are as interchangeable as Yankees and Dodgers; and that most of us live on plantations and talk with a syrupy Magnolia blossom drawl. Nothing could be further from the truth. Ever see the movie *The Big Easy*? Forget everything you saw or heard.

▲ PHILIP GOULD

But we do talk funny. Many of the natives speak a tongue all their own, and not very well. Enunciation and grammar are not our fortes. Most say the accent is similar to what you'd find in Brooklyn. If you drive into a full-service gas station, the attendant might ask, "Check da erl, cap?" Of course, "erl" is oil, "foist" comes before second, "thoid" is where you wind up when you hit a triple, "goils" grow up to be women, and "ya momma" is the lady who changed your diapers. Here, we "ax" questions, "wrench da dishes in da zinc," and "wrap da toikey in tin ferl and baste it wid olive erl." And we routinely put accents on the wrong syllables. Er, da wrong syllables.

ARK TWAIN ONCE WROTE that New Orleans' greatest architecture can be found in its cemeteries. The aboveground vaults in these "cities of the dead" also provide inspiration for local novelist and vampire chronicler Anne Rice (ABOVE).

If you're walking down the street minding your own business and somebody asks you "Where y'at?" don't say "Right here." The term "Where y'at?"
is simply a friendly colloquial salutation that means "How's it going?" or
"How're you doing?" Coined generations ago by inhabitants of two
character-laden blue-collar areas of the city, the Ninth Ward and the Irish
Channel, "Where y'at?" knows no bounds in today's metropolitan area. The
people who use this term are dubbed "Yats"—lovingly by some, disparag-
ingly by others.

While we're on the subject of language and local idiosyncrasies, you
should know that the city is not "New Or-leeenz," as it is frequently pronounced. It's "Noo Awlins" or "N'Awlins," unless you want to stamp yourself
as an outsider. Also, San Francisco has cable cars, and lots of cities have trolleys,
but New Orleans has streetcars. What you might call a median is a "neutral
ground" here. Street names are either French, difficult to pronounce, strange,
impossible to spell, or all of the above. Toulouse. Tchoupitoulas. Terpsichore.
Delachaise. Melpomene. Magazine. Religious. Chef Menteur. Bruxelles.
Pelopidas. Carondelet. And Burgundy, which is pronounced Bur-GUN-dy.

We're also the city of one-way streets, streets that have one name on one side of Canal (the main drag) and another on the other side, and streets with "No Left Turn" signs for miles. New Orleans is a confusing city to learn. There are streets that end abruptly. And we give directions that, well, need a translator: "Ya go tards da river and tree blocks pass Collar-seem Street. Ya go left like ya headin' downtown. Ya gonna pass Tep-sa-coe Street and when ya get to Mel-pa-mean, it's on da Uptown-River corner. Right where dat ol' barroom used to be. I know where it's at cuz ma momma 'n nem stay right across the street next to da snowball stand."

We're also a city not known for drivers with great automotive habits. If the driver in front of you puts on a turn signal, consider yourself lucky. For the most part, just like rearview mirrors, turn signal indicators are used to hang Carnival beads on. And running red lights is such a tradition in New Orleans that one year there was a joke saying the City Council had gotten tough by passing an ordinance that allowed only three motorists to run a stoplight after it turns red, provided they maintain a speed of more than 50 miles per hour.

ANOTHER WORKDAY BEGINS FOR dealcutters and canecutters alike. In the city, businesspeople board the St. Charles streetcar for a rumbly ride downtown. In the country, a day's work may begin and end in rain-soaked sugarcane fields.

F EVERYTHING ABOUT NEW ORLEANS SEEMS confusing, fear not. There *are* a lot of things here that are difficult to understand. But if you visit, don't be intimidated. I have spent more than 50 years in these unique surroundings, am paid to comment on what takes place here, and keep my finger on the pulse of the city. I can honestly tell you that the pulse is abnormal. A lot of what takes place here makes no sense at all, and most of it defies analysis.

But there's never a dull day. Partly because New Orleans is in Louisiana, one of the few states whose legislators—despite all kinds of major issues facing them each year—have found time to name a state fruit, a state

THE LOUISIANA SUPERDOME, which takes center stage in the night skyline, has been compared to everything from the top of a roll-on deodorant bottle to a spaceship. At sunrise, a painted barn may seem just as otherworldy.

hound dog, a state fossil, and a state insect. Just for the record, the state insect is the firefly, which narrowly defeated the mosquito and everyone's sentimental favorite, the roach.

Louisiana and New Orleans politics are infamous, but the state and the city have survived despite them. The legendary Kingfish, the late Governor Huey P. Long, once said, "God help Louisiana if I die. My rascals will steal them blind." And more recently, Governor Edwin W. Edwards, who many thought mistook Las Vegas as the capital of Louisiana, said, "The governors of Oklahoma and Texas, both of them Republicans, they go to

church every day. They have only one wife. They do not gamble. They do not use curse words in public. They are honest, decent men. And it has not helped the economy of Texas or Oklahoma one bit."

Greater New Orleans is home to 1.3 million people, fewer than 500,000 of whom live inside the city limits. The city has more than 360 miles of water and land, some of it indistinguishable. It has eight universities, but only one has a nickname with a water motif: Tulane University, the Green Wave, the oldest university in the city. New Orleans, occasionally known as "The Crescent City," otherwise "The Big Easy," is the smallest big city in the world, and you can virtually get from one end of it to the other in 25 minutes.

A CANOPIED WALK UNDER AN arch of 28 oak trees gives the 1839 Oak Alley plantation its name. A more contemporary view can be had from the Canal Street Ferry Terminal, which overlooks the sleek turquoise-colored Aquarium of the Americas (LEFT).

It's a city where people live in wooden-framed shotgun houses, so named because the doors of all the rooms from front to back are aligned, creating the possibility that a blast from a shotgun would go straight through the house and out the back door. However, this is not widely practiced or recommended. People here sit on "the stoop," not the front steps; when they go grocery shopping, they "make groceries"; and "lagniappe" is something extra given away, like a 13th doughnut with a dozen. If you want lettuce, tomatoes, mayonnaise, and the works on your sandwich, just say you want it "dressed." We drink café au lait, our doughnuts are beignets

(square, with powdered sugar, and without holes), and Dixie Beer is still being brewed. When you buy a po'boy, you get a Barq's—never say root beer.

Our attractions include the world-class Aquarium of the Americas and its stunning IMAX Theater on the river; the heralded Audubon Zoo uptown; the Louisiana Superdome, which is home to the New Orleans Saints; the Fair Grounds Race Course; the New Orleans Museum of Art; the Louisiana Philharmonic Orchestra; the New Orleans Zephyrs Class AAA baseball team; and the aforementioned cemeteries, where imposing tombs and vaults honor everyone from military heroes from the Battle of New Orleans to gamblers, a voodoo queen, and a famed madam of Storyville, the city's once-thriving red-light district.

There are also plantations along the river, nearby swamp tours where you can encounter live alligators, and charter boat fishing. Hunting and fishing, by the way, are huge throughout the state. It's the reason the motto on our license plates is "Sportsman's Paradise." There's also shopping at the Riverwalk, a development along the Mississippi, and in the quaint shops in the French Quarter; antique stores in the Quarter and on Magazine Street; and, obviously, scores of quality restaurants all over the area.

To really get a feel for the city, however, venture out of the tourist areas to the mom-and-pop neighborhood bars and restaurants that really define New Orleans. New Orleans is a barroom city, a gambling town, and a city that likes to talk sports. Since there is a 7-to-1 ratio of bars to churches in the city, and at last count there were 500-plus churches, there are a lot of spots to choose from. Some well-known time-honored establishments (some have live music, others jukeboxes) include Fat Harry's on St. Charles Avenue; Bruno's on Maple Street; the Rendon Inn in Mid City; Cooter Brown's, Mid-City Lanes Rock 'N' Bowl, and Ye Olde College Inn on Carrollton Avenue; Irma Thomas' Lion's Den on Gravier Street; Ernie K-Doe's Mother-in-Law Lounge on North Claiborne; Little People's Place on Barracks Street; the Rivershack Tavern on River Road; the Parkway Tavern on Canal Boulevard; Liuzza's on Bienville Street; F&M Patio Bar on Tchoupitoulas; Igor's on St. Charles Avenue; Le Bon Temps Roule on Magazine; Franky & Johnny's on Arabella; and Whitey's Pool Hall on Downman Road. Before you go, however, check with a native or a hotel employee to see if your choice matches what you're looking for and if you'll be comfortable there.

THE RAUCOUS SOUNDS OF BANDS such as Beau Jocque and the Zydeco Hi-Rollers drown out the crash of bowling pins at Mid-City Lanes (OPPOSITE). On Sunday evenings, Bruce Daigrepont's Cajun dances at Tipitina's (ABOVE) attract two-steppers and waltzers, but no basketball players.

LL THAT SAID, IT IS THE FRENCH QUARTER—with its charming buildings and iron lace balconies, funky music halls, bars, musicians, galleries, artists, antique stores, and restaurants—that not only houses the city's crown jewels, but is the heartbeat of our town, the pièce de résistance, the tour de force. Its value to the city of New Orleans cannot be overstated; it's what sets New Orleans apart. The French and Spanish influences, especially, are everywhere, and they are well preserved. New Orleans is the closest thing to Europe you'll find anywhere in this country, and it reeks with stories waiting to be told.

Some of the best stories come from the colorful buggy drivers who hold sway in the Quarter. Just keep in mind that they are prone to embellish and exaggerate from time to time. Like many of us, they have difficulty separating history and legend, and they rarely let facts stand in the way of a good story. On a tour I was once told that the pirate Jean Laffite, who was much a part of the Battle of New Orleans, rang a bell in a church on St. Charles Avenue to warn somebody that somebody else was coming. Curious, I checked the next day. The church wasn't built until 80 years after the War of 1812. No big deal here. Napoleon, also a part of the lore of New Orleans and a major player in a minor $23 mil-

THERE ARE MANY WAYS TO VIEW the Vieux Carré. Buggy drivers provide "rolling" commentary on the streets and legends of the Quarter from their mule-drawn carriages.

THE VISTA FROM THE TOP OF Jax Brewery stretches to Lake Pontchartrain and recalls the days when the spires of St. Louis (ABOVE AND OPPOSITE) were the city's tallest man-made structures.

lion transaction named the Louisiana Purchase, once said, "History is nothing more than rumors agreed upon."

For my money, the prettiest snapshots of the Quarter are from an elevated vantage point, such as the Jax Brewery rooftop. In one direction, you can see paddle wheelers on the Mississippi, with their calliopes playing. And in the other, you can see Jackson Square, framed by the ancient steeple-topped St. Louis Cathedral. If you blink your eyes and watch the lights twinkle at night as the mule-drawn carriages go by on Decatur Street, and listen to the sweet sounds of a street musician, you'll swear you're in another country.

Know what? You are. ⚜

NEW ORLEANS:

ABOUT 1.3 MILLION RESIDENTS live in metro New Orleans, but it's not always a "bustling" city. Among popular pastimes are leisurely walks, sitting on the front stoop, and reclining on a second-story balcony.

ROLLIN' ON THE RIVER

Ⓝ ew Orleans has as many "characters" as it has street corners, and one of the city's most famous is the man who incorporates hundreds of plastic Mardi Gras beads into his wardrobe (opposite).

Other less noted, but equally entertaining, characters are (clockwise from top left) a woman who looks like she rolled right out of *A Streetcar Named Desire*; the "Chicken Man," who is said to perform voodoo

throughout the French Quarter; a street entertainer who makes the impossible appear to be real; and a cop who could have easily played a part in *The Big Easy*.

E ASEL DOES IT: EACH DAY, ARTISTS
set up shop around Jackson
Square, offering caricatures and pas-
tel portraits. And throughout the
French Quarter, countless numbers
of T-shirt stores hawk wearable art.

Since 1934 the Famous Door has been a Bourbon Street landmark—although most of the famous names who passed through this music club are from decades past. Several other famous musicians don't "rue" the fact that they got their start playing their instruments for tips on French Quarter streets.

T HE SACRED AND THE PROFANE often rub shoulders on Bourbon Street. Strip clubs offer low-tech earthly pleasures, while street preachers make high-tech promises of heavenly rewards.

Built by the Baroness Micaela Almonester Pontalba between 1849 and 1851, the Pontalba apartments are some of the nation's oldest, and the waiting list to rent these Jackson Square dwellings is still the city's longest (OPPOSITE). No longer available, however, is the fabled hallucinogenic drink called absinthe, for which the Old Absinthe House is named (ABOVE).

In 1856 the Place d'Armes (BOTTOM LEFT) was renamed Jackson Square in honor of General Andrew Jackson (RIGHT), who defended the city against the British in the 1815 Battle of New Orleans.

Bordering the park is the Cabildo, the former seat of Spanish power in the city (TOP LEFT). Documents for the Louisiana Purchase were signed here in 1803.

In the 1930s the Works Progress Administration restored much of the Quarter, including the French Market. The Market is the site of the 24-hour farmer's market, which carries fresh local produce and products, as well as the spices that dominate Cajun food.

▶ JONATHAN POSTAL

Tourists can take a leisurely spin through the French Quarter on mule-drawn buggies, which are operated by drivers who spin entertaining (but often historically dubious) tales about such landmarks as the House of the Rising Sun and Pirate's Alley.

Royal Street antique shops are filled with surprises. The expressions on the faces of statues or mannequins seem to suggest untold secrets.

It can be argued in New Orleans more than in any other city that art is subjective. Whether your taste leans toward fine sculpture or more bestial trophies, New Orleans shops can satisfy your needs.

ROLLIN' ON THE RIVER

54

New Orleanians like to have their cake and decorate it too. Evidence of that fact can be best seen in the ornate details of French Quarter architecture.

56

P ATTERNS OF DAILY LIFE CAN BE viewed through ironwork over-looking Jackson Square (OPPOSITE) or through the afternoon shadows that play upon downtown's One Shell Square, the city's tallest office build-ing (ABOVE).

ROLLIN' ON THE RIVER

PICTURESQUE VIEWS ARE PROVIDED by shutters, hanging ferns, passing church shadows, and old cars. Scenes like these are one reason New Orleans is often called the northernmost city of the Caribbean.

BUILT ON ONE OF THE SITES OF THE 1984 World's Fair, the half-mile Riverwalk Marketplace contains more than 200 shops and restaurants. On the river side of the mall is the Spanish Plaza, where a free concert is held each year on the night before Mardi Gras.

Captain Steve Nicoul steers the *Natchez* through the mighty Mississippi. This steamboat stern-wheeler can accommodate up to 1,600 passengers, and it rolls on the river each evening with jazz cruises that feature the Dukes of Dixieland.

THE PORT OF NEW ORLEANS stretches over 15 miles of Mississippi riverfront and is one of the world's most active ports. Every day, river barges and cargo ships chug up Big Muddy to load and unload their wares. Woldenberg Riverfront Park offers picnickers and passersby a leisurely view of this bustling waterway.

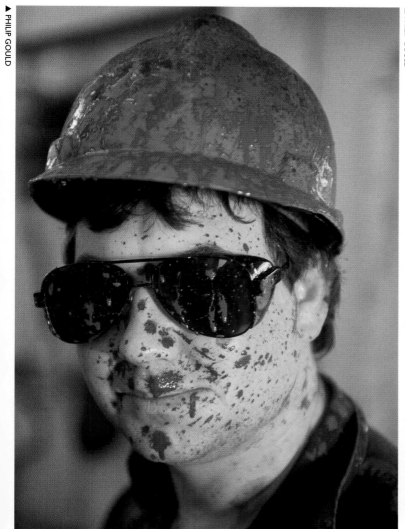

Offshore drilling made New Orleans a major economic player during the oil boom years. The city is still recovering from the drop in oil prices in the 1980s, but outfits such as the Phillip's Sonat Rig continue to mine the Gulf of Mexico for black gold.

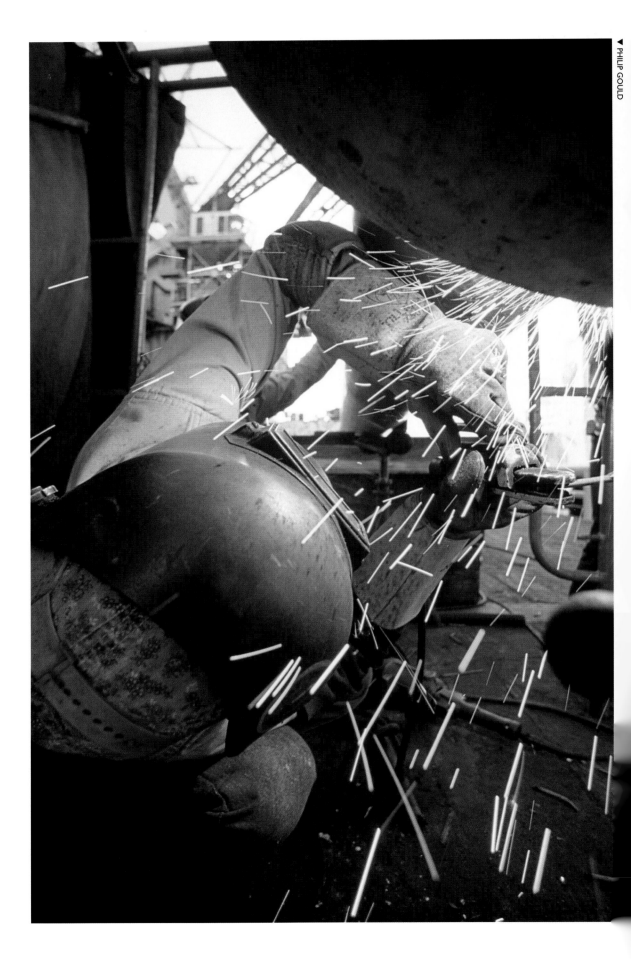

SINCE OFFSHORE WORKERS STAY ON their rigs for weeks at a time, an outdoor barbecue is a popular way to feed the crew.

I**N 1742 SOUTH LOUISIANA'S FIRST** sugar plantation began operations. Refining, storing, loading, and even sweeping the sweetener remains a major industry here. It's for this reason that the annual college football match, held in the Superdome on New Year's Day, is named the Sugar Bowl.

THE OIL INDUSTRY IS MORE THAN pipe dreams. Hard work helps keep the crude flowing through the Murphy Oil Refinery (OPPOSITE) and a Terrebonne Bay offshore rig (ABOVE).

A GLASS-ENCLOSED LOBBY CREATES a sense of open space in the downtown Hilton hotel (OPPOSITE). The past and present find expression in the angles and arches of New Orleans architecture, including the stately U.S. Court of Appeals Building (BOTTOM), which borders Lafayette Park.

NEW ORLEANS

THE CITY'S TRADITION OF ETHNIC diversity can be seen in the statues that surround the 33-story World Trade Center, including Joan of Arc (OPPOSITE) and Bernardo de Galvez (LEFT). Other public art reflects the modern era, like this bronze sculpture, created by Enrique Alferez, which stands outside the Louisiana Land and Exploration Building (RIGHT).

ALTHOUGH THE ST. LOUIS Cathedral offers daily tours, the historic church is still the home of an active parish and holds regular services. New Orleans Archbishop Francis Schulte consoles mourners during a funeral mass, and a statue of Christ, adorned with a symbol of the city's lighter side, welcomes worshipers with open arms.

DATING TO 1734, THE OLD Ursuline Convent is the oldest building in the French Quarter (OPPOSITE TOP). Examples of other long-standing Catholic traditions are these St. Joseph's Day altars laden with ornately braided bread and other edible delights (TOP; OPPOSITE BOTTOM), and the annual St. Patrick's Day mass at St. Mary's church (BOTTOM).

Iᴛ's ɴᴏᴛ ᴇᴀsʏ ʙᴇɪɴɢ ɢʀᴇᴇɴ,
indeed. When the festive St.
Patrick's Day parade rolls up the
Irish Channel neighborhood, beads,
cabbages, and potatoes are tossed to
the crowds. Local politicians also get
into the act, including Mayor Marc
Morial (ʙᴏᴛᴛᴏᴍ ʟᴇꜰᴛ).

AMONG THE CHALLENGES FACING Police Superintendent Richard Pennington (OPPOSITE TOP) and Mayor Morial (OPPOSITE BOTTOM) is restoring public trust in the NOPD. Perhaps the most trusted woman in local political history is former Congresswoman Lindy Boggs (LEFT); she's also the mother of journalist Cokie Roberts.

Sister Helen Prejean (OPPO-SITE) and Matt Suarez (ABOVE) are well-known local political activists who are revered for their work with area children. Prejean gained national fame when her book, *Dead Man Walking*, was turned into a Hollywood movie.

NEW ORLEANS:

Iɴ ᴀᴅᴅɪᴛɪᴏɴ ᴛᴏ Lᴏʏᴏʟᴀ Univer-sity (ᴏᴘᴘᴏꜱɪᴛᴇ), several fine private and public universities call New Or-leans home, including (ᴄʟᴏᴄᴋᴡɪꜱᴇ ꜰʀᴏᴍ ᴛᴏᴘ ʟᴇꜰᴛ) Tulane, Dillard, Uni-versity of New Orleans, and Xavier.

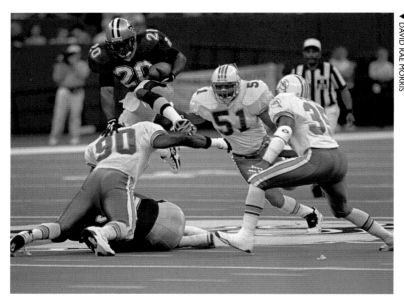

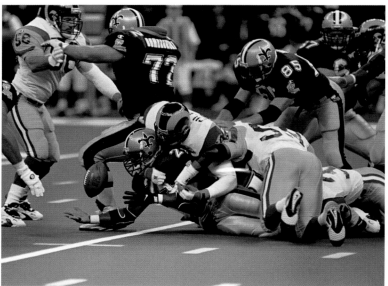

THE NEW ORLEANS SAINTS, WHO play at the much-talked-about Superdome, are one reason that Louisiana has been called a Sportsman's Paradise. The team is still searching for another kicker like Tom Dempsey (RIGHT), who has held the league record for longest field goal (63 yards) since 1970.

A LSO PLAYED AT THE SUPERDOME is the annual Bayou Classic, in which Southern University faces Grambling University's longtime coach, Eddie Robinson, who is shown here with renowned sportscaster Ahmad Rashad (TOP LEFT).

For basketball fans, the University of New Orleans features exciting action from both its women's and men's teams, which play home games at Kiefer Uno Lakefront Arena.

"I WENT ON DOWN TO THE AUDUBON Zoo, and they all asked for you . . ." This popular local song was inspired by one of the nation's loveliest zoos. You can walk to the zoo through the 340-acre Audubon Park, a popular weekend destination for families and golfers. Some of the mighty trees in Audubon Park's Oak Alley (PAGES 94 AND 95) may hark back to the years when the plot of land belonged to Jean-Baptiste Le Moyne, the founder of New Orleans.

PAGES 94 AND 95: PHILIP GOULD

ᴎ ATURE ASSERTS ITSELF IN COUNT-
less forms—some more un-
usual than others. An iron fence is no
match for these aggressive old trees
(OPPOSITE). And the uniform weave
of palm bark provides one example
of the lush tropical vegetation that's
found in the Crescent City (ABOVE).

Attractive single-family houses line New Orleans' historic streets as well as such waterways as Bayou St. John, which leads to Lake Pontchartrain. Each day, walking tours explore the antebellum splendor of the Garden District.

ALL MANNER OF AUGUST COLUMNS can be seen in the manors along St. Charles Avenue. These stately architectural features are also the namesake for the Columns Hotel (LEFT); this 1884 structure was featured in the film *Pretty Baby*.

If the Doullout Steamboat Houses (OPPOSITE TOP) look like ships, that's because they were constructed at the turn of the century by a husband-and-wife team of river pilots. Local architecture can be lavish or simple; narrow shotgun houses are named for a single row of rooms through which one could fire a shotgun.

E IGHT ACRES OF GARDENS AND
fountains surround the Longue
Vue House in the suburb of Metairie
(OPPOSITE). West Indies-style architecture is featured in the Pitot House,
which is located at Bayou St. John,
on the site of the city's first French
settlement (ABOVE).

Tours are available of the 1839 Oak Alley house (OPPO-SITE) as well as the interiors of many Garden District homes (ABOVE); Oak Alley's 28 columns were designed to match the number of oak trees on the estate.

NEW ORLEANS:

THE OAKS AT OAK ALLEY ARE UP to three centuries old. The former plantation now offers both tours and overnight accommodations.

A VARIETY OF ARCHITECTURAL styles can be seen in the plantation homes that line the Mississippi River. The Greek Revival Houmas House is framed by oaks and formal gardens (OPPOSITE). The palatial Nottoway Plantation (ABOVE) features details of both Greek Revival and Italianate styles, and includes a spectacular white ballroom.

ONE LOCAL ATTRACTION SPIRALS into another in views of a staircase at Houmas House (OPPOSITE) and the modern exterior of the Aquarium of the Americas (ABOVE).

New Orleans features amenities for people of all ages and interests. Among the Big Easy's most popular venues for family outings are City Park, Aquarium of the Americas, and Louisiana Children's Museum, where kids can get positively bubbly. On Loyola Avenue the triumph of the human spirit is celebrated in a work of sculpture that honors cancer survivors.

A FREE OUTDOOR GALLERY OF wall art showcases wild things, archaelogical finds, eerily lifelike clarinets, and seductive gators. Meanwhile, a row of colorfully painted second liners rests up before the big show at Jazz Fest.

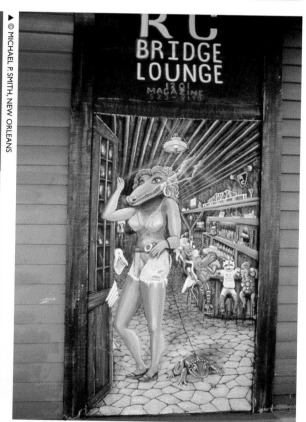

MAGAZINE STREET, WHICH takes its name from the French word for "shop," is a major thoroughfare for art and antiques. It's also a favorite destination for Tulane and Loyola students looking to hit—or avoid—the books.

AMONG THE PUBLIC SPACES that feature work by sculptor John Scott (TOP) is the Riverwalk (BOTTOM); to see Ida Kohlmeyer's creations, take a downtown stroll on Poydras Street (OPPOSITE TOP). Located in City Park, the New Orleans Museum of Art (OPPOSITE BOTTOM) has a permanent collection of classic and modern works; highlights include pre-Columbian art and an exhibit of Fabergé eggs.

Louisiana waterways reflect the nightly sunset. The expansive Lake Pontchartrain measures 40 miles long by 25 miles wide and is crossed by the nearly-24-mile-long Causeway (OPPOSITE).

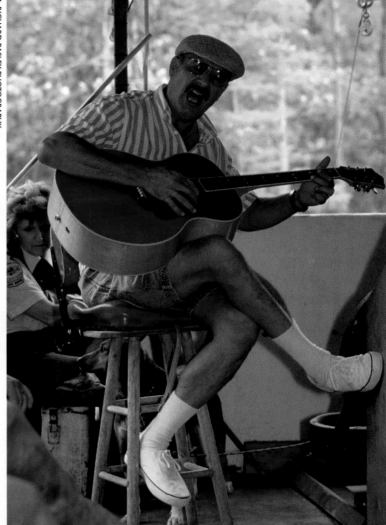

F OLKS IN THE BAYOU CONSIDER visitors to the area a delight: You'll never get an icy reception in the small towns that dot south Louisiana. Tours into bayou country feature such singing guides as Black Guidry, or "Cajun Man" (RIGHT); 12-foot alligators hungry for a snack; and swamps, swamps, and more swamps (PAGES 128 AND 129).

PAGES 128 AND 129: PHILIP GOULD

T HERE ARE MANY WAYS TO LIVE off the fat of the water. Shrimp boats cruise the Houma Navigational Canal, while fishermen mine the bayous for crabs and alligators, which are snared with baited poles.

A WALKWAY LEADING TO A HIDDEN cabin reveals how rural Louisianians have adapted to life on the omnipresent bayous and rivers. In the mossy wilderness outside New Orleans, stubby cypress roots called "knees" decorate the water's surface.

OUT IN CAJUN COUNTRY, THE
French Quarter seems as distant as a foreign country. Avery
Island (OPPOSITE BOTTOM) is home to
flocks of egrets that nest in a man-
made sanctuary called Bird City.
Meanwhile, a young competitor
practices for the day when he, too,
can be a crack quacker bagger.

MANY RURAL ROADHOUSES BEAR the names of their owners; others recall a particularly notorious statewide election.

T HE SMALL TOWN OF GRAMERCY, located west of New Orleans, hosts a dramatic Christmas tradition: the lighting of bonfires to guide Papa Noel along the Mississippi River. Locals spend many hours cutting, hauling, and building in preparation for the event.

PHILIP GOULD

FESTIVITIES LIGHT UP NEW Orleans year-round. Each December a seasonal display brings electric-powered angels to City Park. Candles are placed on area tombs for All Saints' Day and are cradled in hands for Christmas Eve caroling in Jackson Square.

BELIEVERS SUCH AS THE PRIESTESS Yaffi (OPPOSITE) still practice the religion of voodoo, a spiritual merging of African, Caribbean, and Catholic traditions. At the House of Voodoo, a painting of Marie Laveau (LEFT) honors the 19th-century New Orleans "voodoo queen."

NEW ORLEANS:

New Orleans' best-known contemporary author is vampire chronicler Anne Rice, who resides (with her extensive doll collection) in the Garden District.

In
memory of
FRANK FRITCH.
Died N 21 198
Age y

THE DECAY OF OLD CEMETERIES provides a chilling reminder of the work of time, as does a mysterious stairway that appears to lead to the hereafter.

Cemeteries hold a mystical charm for New Orleanians. At Saint Roch Cemetery, for example, visitors are invited to hang a symbol of their ailment in hopes of being cured. Those who have eye problems often turn to Saint Lucy, the patron saint of vision, whose eyes were restored after being torn out of their sockets.

D ue to the area's swampy land, aboveground "burial" became a necessary tradition in New Orleans. With fences built around concrete vaults, these plots resemble small neighborhoods.

Traditional jazz funerals, like the one for musician Danny Barker (OPPOSITE), comfort the living and serenade the departed into the "sweet by-and-by."

THROUGHOUT THE FRENCH Quarter, street musicians of every stripe rely on their talents and the generosity of passersby. One young, but already legendary, local musician is Troy "Trombone Shorty" Andrews, who draws a crowd wherever he plays.

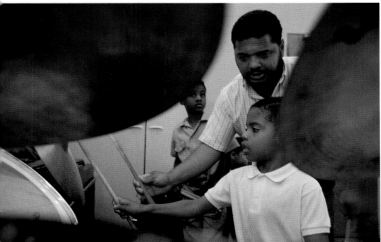

ACH NIGHT, PRESERVATION
Hall presents some of the finest
practitioners of traditional jazz.
One beloved player who has passed
through these doors is trumpeter
Percy Humphrey (OPPOSITE BOTTOM
RIGHT).

The next generation of jazz, ably
led by Trombone Shorty (TOP),
promises to carry on New Orleans'
rich muscial heritage. Local educators
Kidd Jordan (BOTTOM RIGHT) and
Jonathan Bloom (BOTTOM LEFT), who
is shown here with his son Jonathan
Jr., are also keeping jazz alive in
the city.

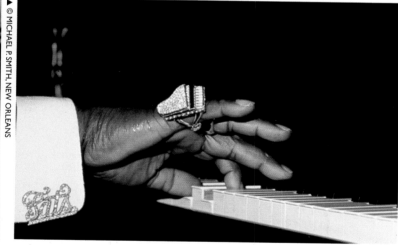

P LAYERS PAST AND PRESENT contribute to New Orleans' reputation as America's most musical city. Among the brightest luminaries are (CLOCKWISE FROM OPPOSITE TOP) the Neville Brothers, Harry Connick Jr., Dr. John, Fats Domino, Professor Longhair, Pete Fountain, and Wynton Marsalis.

Ⲛamed for a song by Professor Longhair, Tipitina's (opposite) is one of the city's most popular music halls. Nighthawks also soar to hear (clockwise from top left) jazzmen and reggae gurus at Cafe Brasil; local favorites, the Iguanas, at Mid-City Bowling Lanes; modern jazz maestros at Snug Harbor; and some of New Orleans' favorite sons, the Neville Brothers, at the House of Blues.

NEW ORLEANS

E ACH YEAR, THE 10-DAY NEW ORLEANS Jazz & Heritage Festival attracts a half-million music lovers and pumps $200 million into the local economy. Local and national performers have included (OPPOSITE CLOCKWISE FROM TOP LEFT) Al Green, the Louisiana Aces, Ray Charles, the Guardians of the Flame Mardi Gras Indians, Fats Domino, Walter "Wolfman" Washington, Chuck Berry, and Charles and Charmaine Neville. And there are just as many different ways to listen and dance as there are styles of music.

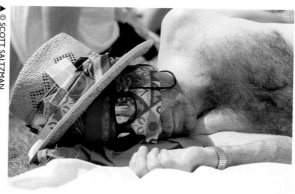

▶ JONATHAN POSTAL

▶ RICHARD PASLEY PHOTOGRAPHY

Each year, Big Chief Percy Lewis of the Black Eagles (OPPO-SITE) hand-sews a new Mardi Gras Indian suit. These finely detailed costumes have been recognized as an important example of folk art and are displayed in museums around the world. Dressed in red (TOP LEFT) is the legendary Big Chief Jolly, uncle to the Neville Brothers.

IN THE WEEKS PRECEDING MARDI
Gras, parades roll through the
streets day and night. After dark, the
extravagant floats are often lit by
flambeaux carriers, who fuel the
flames with tanks of gas.

Mardi Gras is an established tradition of festivities in the Crescent City, featuring parades, hordes of people, and a whole lot of fun. Crowds catch plastic beads and gold doubloons at such parades as Rex, which since 1872 has reigned as King of Carnival. Revelers trade the beads for various "favors," while professional musicians (that's Pete Fountain with the clarinet) and impromptu bands of amateurs perform in the streets.

New Orleans:

C ROWDS MAY LUNGE FORWARD FOR doubloons, but the most-prized parade catch during Mardi Gras is the hand-painted Zulu coconut.

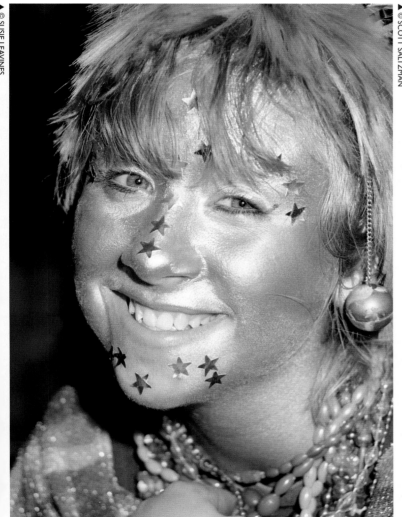

Faces make fine canvases, but for serious cartooning, there's "no place like dome."

A FTER THE PARADES, COSTUMERS
flock to the French Quarter,
where celebrants fly their own colors.

P OP CULTURE MAINSTAYS SUCH AS Elvis Presley join irreverently treated religious icons for Mardi Gras. The day can be both bawdy fun and a family outing.

CARNIVAL IS A SWIRL OF SIGHTS and sounds that must be seen— and heard—to be believed.

At Jazz Fest and Mardi Gras, our reach may exceed our grasp, but we always raise our arms in celebration.

City Council member Peggy Wilson (TOP) joins a parade of kissers in proving that ours is a most romantic city.

The "Wishman" is a familiar sight in the French Quarter, selling—of course—wishes. And on Mardi Gras, the Crescent itself joins the parade through the Crescent City.

If you're feeling lucky, you can try a hot dog from a vendor that was immortalized in John Kennedy Toole's novel *A Confederacy of Dunces.* Even luckier is a link of encased rice and meat that's called *boudin,* displayed here by Mrs. Ellis Cormier.

▶ JONATHAN POSTAL

▶ PHILIP GOULD

IN NEW ORLEANS, OUR RESTAURANTS are our theaters, and the chefs and owners are the stars of the show. Among the best are Brennan's, which made breakfast an art form (OPPOSITE LEFT), and K-Paul's, where chef Paul Prudhomme specializes in blackened cuisine (OPPOSITE RIGHT). Other notables are (CLOCKWISE FROM TOP LEFT) Emeril Lagasse of Emeril's, Ruth Fertel of Ruth's Chris Steak House, Justin Galatoire Frey and David Gooch of Galatoire's, and Bayona's Susan Spicer.

S OME OF THE TASTES OF NEW Orleans not to be missed include oysters on the half shell at Acme's (TOP AND BOTTOM RIGHT), fresh bread at La Madeleine (CENTER LEFT), and delicious pralines at The Praline Connection (BOTTOM LEFT).

Oᴛʜᴇʀ ʟᴏᴄᴀʟ ᴛʀᴇᴀᴛs ɪɴᴄʟᴜᴅᴇ (ᴄʟᴏᴄᴋᴡɪsᴇ ғʀᴏᴍ ᴛᴏᴘ ʟᴇғᴛ) blackened fish at K-Paul's, a Pimm's Cup at the Napoleon House, turtle soup at Commander's Palace, and bananas Foster at Brennan's.

THE MENU IS SHORT AND SWEET
at the 24-hour Café Du Monde:
powdered-sugar-drenched beignets
and creamy café au lait.

As the river keeps on rolling, the sun sets gently over French Quarter streets, Riverwalk joggers, refinery workers, and even an alligator in repose.

PAGES 198 AND 199: RICHARD PASLEY PHOTOGRAPHY

PROFILES IN EXCELLENCE

A LOOK AT THE CORPORATIONS, BUSINESSES, PROFESSIONAL GROUPS, AND COMMUNITY SERVICE ORGANIZATIONS THAT HAVE MADE THIS BOOK POSSIBLE. THEIR STORIES—OFFERING AN INFORMAL CHRONICLE OF THE LOCAL BUSINESS COMMUNITY—ARE ARRANGED ACCORDING TO THE DATE THEY WERE ESTABLISHED IN THE NEW ORLEANS AREA.

ANTOINE'S RESTAURANT ❖ BISSO TOWBOAT COMPANY, INC. ❖ BURKS-FARBER CLINICS ❖ CAFÉ DU MONDE ❖ CENTURY GRAPHICS CORPORATION ❖ DIXIE WEB GRAPHIC CORPORATION ❖ DOUBLETREE HOTEL • NEW ORLEANS ❖ EYE SURGERY CENTER OF LOUISIANA ❖ GERTRUDE GARDNER, REALTORS ❖ HOLIDAY INN DOWNTOWN-SUPERDOME ❖ HARRY KELLEHER & CO., INC. ❖ L&L OIL COMPANY ❖ MAGNOLIA MARKETING COMPANY ❖ M.G. MAHER & COMPANY, INC. ❖ MARKS PAPER COMPANY ❖ MONTGOMERY, STIRE & PARTNERS ❖ THE NEW ORLEANS BOARD OF TRADE, LTD. ❖ NEW ORLEANS HILTON RIVERSIDE ❖ NEW ORLEANS LIMOUSINE SERVICE ❖ NEW ORLEANS MARRIOTT ❖ NEW ORLEANS MEDICAL COMPLEX ❖ NEW ORLEANS MUSEUM OF ART ❖ PORT OF NEW ORLEANS ❖ ROYAL SONESTA HOTEL AND CHATEAU SONESTA HOTEL ❖ SAZERAC COMPANY, INC. ❖ SIGMA COATINGS ❖ STEWART & STEVENSON SERVICES, INC. ❖ UNIVERSITY OF NEW ORLEANS ❖ WASTE MANAGEMENT OF NEW ORLEANS ❖ WHITNEY NATIONAL BANK ❖ WILLIAMS & ASSOCIATES ARCHITECTS ❖ WWL-TV, CHANNEL 4

PHOTO: PHILIP GOULD

1830-1949

1830
Sazerac Company, Inc.

1840
Antoine's Restaurant

1862
Café Du Monde

1880
The New Orleans Board
of Trade, Ltd.

1883
Whitney National Bank

1890
Bisso Towboat Company,
Inc.

PHOTO: PHILIP GOULD

SAZERAC COMPANY, INC.

THE NEW ORLEANS-BASED SAZERAC COMPANY, INC., IS ONE OF the largest independent producers and importers of beverages in the United States. The firm traces its existence to 1830, when Sewell Taylor converted his Merchants Exchange Coffee House at 16 Royal Street into a retail liquor store and became an importer of brandies from the French firm of Sazerac des Forge et Fils.

STEEPED IN HISTORY

In 1849 John B. Schiller acquired the establishment, named it the Sazerac Coffee House, and struck up an acquaintance with Antoine Peychaud, who owned an apothecary on Royal Street. Peychaud's most prized possession was a secret family recipe for aromatic bitters, which he used to make a delightful brandy concoction that he often shared with friends and acquaintances. Through the collaboration of Schiller and Peychaud, the now-famous Sazerac Cocktail was introduced commercially, making New Orleans home to the world's first cocktail.

Following Schiller's death in 1869, a former employee named Thomas H. Handy became the establishment's proprietor, and the name was shortened to Sazerac House. Handy purchased the Peychaud Bitters recipe and began making the Sazerac Cocktail with American rye whiskeys rather than brandies. In the 1890s Handy began to produce and market a bottled version of the Sazerac Cocktail.

BOOM YEARS

The Sazerac House survived the Prohibition years (1920-1933) by operating for a time as a grocery and then as a delicatessen. In 1948

Sazerac Company's product line features a roster of local favorites, including Herbsaint, Antoine Peychaud's aromatic bitters, and the world's only authentic Sazerac Cocktail (top).

Sazerac Company, Inc., traces its existence to 1830, when Sewell Taylor converted his Merchants Exchange Coffee House at 16 Royal Street into a retail liquor store and became an importer of brandies from the French firm of Sazerac des Forge et Fils (bottom).

of microbrewed beer with Pelican Amber and Pelican Light beers. Sazerac also has begun to explore the vast marketing and distribution potential of China via the development of a sales office called Concorde Holdings based in Beijing.

Although the Sazerac Company has attained great national and international success, it has never forgotten that its home is in New Orleans. The company prides itself on being the largest tax generator in Louisiana and actively supports local charities and civic endeavors. Its product line features a roster of local favorites, including Herbsaint, Praline Liqueur, Antoine Peychaud's aromatic bitters, and the world's only authentic Sazerac Cocktail.

Stephen Goldring and Malcolm Woldenberg acquired Sazerac and led the company to attain rapid growth following its introduction of Taaka Vodka. Since then, Sazerac has produced, marketed, and imported numerous other familiar brand names, including Aspen Glacial Liqueur, Black & White Scotch, and nine brands from Seagram. The greatest surge in the company's growth—a phenomenal 400 percent—has occurred in the years since 1986, despite a simultaneous decline in national per capita alcohol consumption.

Today the Sazerac Company is located in 300,000-square-foot facilities in New Orleans, including a 200,000-square-foot production and distribution center on the banks of the Mississippi River. The company has 360 wholesalers/distributors serving all 50 states, and Sazerac products can be found on the shelves of retailers in more than 40 nations around the world.

The secret to Sazerac's success, says current President Peter W.H. Bordeaux, is niche marketing, a strategy that relies heavily on building brand-name recognition on a very region-specific basis. "We're prepared to build brands on a market basis, whether that market is a region, a state, or one or two cities," he says.

Variety has contributed to Sazerac's strength. In the 1990s the company has had great success handling wines and even such non-traditional products as root beer and schnapps. In 1995 the company responded to the sudden popularity

ANTOINE'S RESTAURANT

NEW ORLEANS' PREMIER RESTAURANT DID NOT BECOME WORLD RENOWNED because of the 1948 best-selling novel *Dinner at Antoine's*; rather author Frances Parkinson Keyes chose Antoine's Restaurant for the title role precisely because it was already a household name. She dedicated the book to its third-generation proprietor, Roy Alciatore, and the 1840 Room—where her story opens and draws to its conclusion—is still as it was when she wrote her description: quaint and well-appointed, the famous old duck press in its place. Today, a mint-condition copy of the novel bearing the restaurant's name is proudly displayed under glass.

FIVE GENERATIONS

The 1840 Room, with its portraits of Antoine and Julie Alciatore and their descendants, commemorates the year when Antoine, a classically trained prodigy already known in France for his culinary creations, arrived in New Orleans and opened a boarding house in today's 600 block of St. Louis Street. The reputation and aromas of his "board" were soon attracting large followings, so in 1860 he moved to a larger building on St. Peter Street. In 1868 Antoine's Restaurant found a permanent home back on St. Louis Street in a prime location between Royal and Bourbon.

Jules Alciatore, only 12 when his father died, apprenticed at Antoine's for six years before he traveled to France for further training in the great kitchens of Strasbourg, Paris, and Marseilles. After returning to New Orleans in 1887, he became chef at the Pickwick Club for a brief period, but he soon took the reins at Antoine's where he gained fame by combining the classic French methods of his father with the unique flavors of Louisiana to create his tantalizing soups and sauces, his often-imitated Oysters Rockefeller, his famed *pompano en papillote*, and dozens of other dishes.

Jules Alciatore's son Roy became proprietor in 1934 and remained through World War II and into the 1950s and 1960s. His sister Marie Louise married William Guste, and their sons William Jr., a longtime attorney general of Louisiana, and Roy Guste Sr. became the fourth-generation proprietors. Roy Guste Jr. followed in 1975, presenting the

SOME OF THE TREASURES TO BE FOUND AT ANTOINE'S RESTAURANT INCLUDE THE 165-FOOT WINE CELLAR, WITH ITS 20,000 BOTTLES (BOTTOM LEFT).

ANTOINE'S HAS BECOME FAMOUS FOR DISHES SUCH AS POMPANO PONCHARTRAIN (BOTTOM RIGHT) THAT COMBINE CLASSIC FRENCH COOKING METHODS WITH THE UNIQUE FLAVORS OF LOUISIANA.

world with the long-awaited *Antoine's Restaurant Cookbook* in 1978.

It is the combination of skills, ingredients, and dedication to service—Old World with New—that forms the basis of Antoine's grand tradition in New Orleans. The restaurant's legacy of cuisine and service has been preserved and cared for lovingly and tenaciously by the same family for 156 years. Each generation has been gifted with the passion and genius to perpetuate the tradition while also adding fresh infusions of its own creativity. "The grandest of all feasts has yet to be served, the greatest dish has yet to be prepared, the finest of wines may still be on the vine," says Bernard Guste, today's fifth-generation proprietor.

WHO'S WHO GUEST BOOK

If New Orleans is the capital of haute cuisine in America, then Antoine's is its capitol. It's the place where United States presidents have dined (including five while in office), and from which seven senior waiters were dispatched to serve Pope John Paul II at the bishop's residence in 1987. The restaurant has served such notables as Jackie Kennedy, Joe Montana, Walt Disney, Walter Annenberg, Mickey Mantle, Theodor S. Geisel (Dr. Seuss), William Faulkner, Jackie Gleason,

Audrey Meadows, Shirley Temple, and Tom Hanks. In 1892 John L. Sullivan and Gentleman Jim Corbett dined at Antoine's while both were in town to duke it out for the world boxing championship, and in 1949 the Duke and Duchess of Windsor banqueted during their Mardi Gras visit.

So many celebrities dined at Antoine's in the glamorous years of the early 20th century that a souvenir booklet was created featuring names such as Pershing, Patton, and Crown Prince Achille Murat of Naples (who settled in Baton Rouge for a time in the 1830s), as well as celebrities of sports, stage, film, music, literature, and aviation. However, says Bernard Guste, "The most important person ever to dine at Antoine's is you."

NEW ORLEANS IS ANTOINE'S, ANTOINE'S IS NEW ORLEANS

Patrons are encouraged to be adventurous in ordering, trust their waiters, and take time to explore the premises beyond the original Main Dining Room. Some of the treasures to be found include the 165-foot wine cellar—with its 20,000 bottles—portraits, art, and various collections displayed in hallways and other dining rooms. There's the cozy "Last Room," which was created in 1949 by converting the building's

stables into a dining room; the Rex Room with royal portraits; the Proteus Queen's Room with its Carnival memorabilia; the Escargot Society Room with its snail carving and sketches by the late editorial cartoonist John Chase, who cofounded the exclusive *Société des Escargots Orleanais*; the Large Annex Room; the Dungeon; and Mystery Room, where the prohibitions of Prohibition were, shall we say, prohibited. Upstairs are the Veranda, Art Gallery Room with its decoratively painted ceiling, Capitol Room with its mahogany paneling from the Old State Capitol, and Japanese Room with its Madame Butterfly decor. The old complex of halls, stairs, hidden warming kitchens, and 15 dining rooms is far more than can be explored in a single visit.

Head chef John Deville has been at Antoine's for 35 years, and all waiters are accomplished in pleasing their guests. There's something for anyone and everyone on the menu, from the soufflé potatoes to sizzling Oysters Rockefeller. Every soup and sauce is a work of art, and traditional New Orleans entrées served at Antoine's represent the standard by which critics will forever rate the city's other great restaurants.

CLOCKWISE FROM TOP: ANTOINE'S HAS SERVED ITS FAMOUS SOUFFLÉ POTATOES (PICTURED FAR LEFT) FOR 150 YEARS. THE RENOWNED OYSTERS ROCKEFELLER, OYSTERS THERMIDOR, AND OYSTERS BIENVILLE WERE ALL CREATED AT ANTOINE'S.

PATRONS WHO DINE AT ANTOINE'S ARE ENCOURAGED TO BE ADVENTUROUS IN ORDERING, TRUST THEIR WAITERS, AND TAKE TIME TO EXPLORE THE PREMISES.

THE COZY "LAST ROOM" WAS CREATED IN THE YEAR 1949 BY CONVERTING THE BUILDING'S STABLES INTO A DINING ROOM.

FROM THE GATES OF JACKSON SQUARE OR ATOP THE FLOOD WALL STEPS THAT lead to the river, Café Du Monde appears to be a series of canvas and masonry arches. On closer review, the structure is always occupied with the sounds and aromas that fill the French Market. Patrons constantly come and go as trayfuls of steaming coffee and smoking beignets arrive and vanish. Conversations hang just over the tabletops, rising and falling in

their own rhythms despite the efforts of street musicians beyond the door.

It's more than masonry, more than human activity. Café Du Monde is a symbol of New Orleans. The crowd of patrons at Café Du Monde is a constant, swelling and ebbing with the clock. Fashionwise, the fabric weight of apparel might change a bit with weather patterns, but season to season the mix of casual clothes, business suits, and formal wear remains steady, with occasional flurries

of Mardi Gras costumes, St. Patrick's green, prom gowns, and colors that mark other special occasions. The procession continues without interruption 24 hours a day, 364 days a year until cathedral bells beyond the square sound the call to midnight Mass on Christmas Eve. Then and only then do the crowds depart, and Café Du Monde goes dark for its only holiday of the year.

This particular segment of the French Market was built in 1813 when the 1791 original was flattened by a hurricane. Café Du Monde was born as a coffee stand in 1862. The enterprise was purchased in 1942 by Hubert Nicholas Fernandez, who at that time was the owner of the Fernandez Wine Cellar located just across Decatur in the Lower Pontalba Building. The family of Hubert Fernandez remains the owner of Café Du Monde to this day.

Hubert Fernandez adopted the 24-hour café schedule to serve the French Market vendors by night and

patrons by day. He ran his wine cellar and coffee shop with the help of his sister Nora, and in 1946 she married Wilbur Schwarz, who also joined the business. Always a strongly family-oriented operation, Fernandez's daughters, sons-in-law, and grandchildren and their spouses have been recruited over the years in various capacities at Café Du Monde.

When Fernandez acquired Café Du Monde, it extended only "two arches" into the French Market, but it quickly expanded with the addition

of a large green-and-white-striped open-air awning that first catches the eye of visitors. The old wine cellar was sold in 1971 in order to clear the decks for concentration on widening the market for Café Du Monde and its products. Soon after, the family began boxing its beignet mix and canning its ground coffee for guests who wanted to take the flavors home.

The beloved beignet (which simply means "fried dough") is known officially as the State Doughnut of Louisiana and has been served since the early days of the original coffee stand. The mix, which involves a secret dough recipe, continues to be blended by the hands of family members. The beignets are served piping hot in orders of three and are lavishly covered with powdered sugar.

The coffee has always begun with a variety of beans from around the world, thus living up to Café Du Monde's name, literally "Coffee of the World," and for years it was painstakingly blended by the family itself. It's now produced by specialists, although still blended to the family's undeviating taste. Once the coffee blend is precise, there's still the matter of the exact darkness of the roast and proper proportion of chicory (the roots of endive plants imported from Belgium, France, and Poland) to ensure the recognizable traits of true Café Du Monde coffee. Nothing less would deserve the proud and precise name that appears on the can: "Café Du Monde Original French Market Coffee Stand Coffee and Chicory." At the café, brewing is a precise procedure that shields the coffee from direct heat to prevent a burned flavor. The coffee is served black or as traditional café au lait, with scalded milk swirled into the pitch-black brew.

Café Du Monde products are popular items at two family-owned gift shops on Decatur Street. One is named Grandad's General Store in honor of Hubert Fernandez, and the other, Uncle Wilbur's Emporium in honor of Wilbur Schwarz. The shops also offer a selection of New Orleans souvenirs. The Fernandez family has developed a color catalog, an 800 number, and a World Wide Web home page for those who wish to have coffee, beignet mix, mugs, and other novelty items delivered to their homes.

The most recent development for this well-established enterprise has been its spread beyond the French Market. Other area locations include the New Orleans Centre, the Riverwalk and Esplanade, and the Oakwood and Lakeside malls, in addition to a location in Atlanta. Café Du Monde has even expanded internationally with more than 50 cafés in Japan, which were a direct result of exposure during the 1984 Louisiana World Exposition. The Japanese cafés are true to the Decatur Street traditions in flavor and appearance.

As the seasons come and go in New Orleans, Café Du Monde will always remain one of the city's most memorable landmarks. Having served its famous coffee and beignets for more than 130 years, the café will continue to charm visitors and patrons both locally and internationally as its influence spreads around the globe.

CLOCKWISE FROM TOP: WILBUR SCHWARZ (RIGHT) IS PICTURED HERE WITH A BEIGNET CHEF INSIDE THE KITCHEN OF CAFÉ DU MONDE IN 1965. THE OUTSIDE PATIO SEATING AREA CAN BE SEEN THROUGH THE WINDOW.

CAFÉ DU MONDE COFFEE AND CHICORY IS AVAILABLE THROUGH MAIL ORDER CATALOGS AND THE COMPANY'S WORLD WIDE WEB PAGE.

IN THE EARLY 1950S CUSTOMERS WERE SERVED IN THEIR CARS THROUGH THE CAFÉ'S CURBSIDE SERVICE. MANY NEW ORLEANIANS REMEMBER SITTING IN THEIR PARENTS' CARS EATING POWDERY BEIGNETS IN THEIR PAJAMAS.

TODAY THE LARGE GREEN-AND-WHITE-STRIPED OPEN-AIR AWNING OF CAFÉ DU MONDE IS AN EYE-CATCHER FOR VISITORS.

PORT OF NEW ORLEANS

HE PORT OF NEW ORLEANS HAS BEEN AROUND LONGER THAN THE CIT of New Orleans. In fact, the port began in 1698 when Pierre Le Moyn Sieur De Iberville, and his teenaged brother Jean-Baptiste Le Moyne, Sieu De Bienville, disembarked at the riverfront of the future French settlemen Following the Native Americans overland to Bayou St. John, Bienville didn return to found the city of New Orleans until 1718. ❧ The port's impact o

the continent's interior was powerful, and it grew with the spread of commerce throughout North America and beyond. Its historical significance extends to the entire nation, as it was a sudden refusal by the later Spanish officials in New Orleans to receive upriver goods that led to the Louisiana Purchase in 1803. Later the Union understood the strategic and economic value of the Confederacy's port of New Orleans only too well, and the early capture of the city in 1862 by Admiral David G. Farragut was a crucial event in the Civil War. By 1870 New Orleans was again handling as much tonnage as ever, and that was just the beginning.

A CENTURY OF GROWTH
Today the port is managed by the Board of Commissioners of the Port of New Orleans, which was created on July 9, 1896, to set policy, regulate traffic, and staff the port's daily operations. By 1996, its centennial year, the board could boast one of the

world's most efficient ports, with wharves and terminals spanning 22 miles of waterfront.

More important than mere size, however, is the port's title of the nation's most intermodal shipping facility. The port offers an easy interchange of cargoes between 70 steamship lines, 16 barge lines, six rail lines, and 75 truck lines. Some 2,400 vessels deliver and receive 30 million tons of cargo each year at the port's 22 million square feet of handling areas and 7.5 million square feet of covered storage areas. These activities provide more than 51,000 local jobs while generating $6 billion in spending and $261 million in state and local taxes annually.

DYNAMIC DECADE
Under the guidance of President and Chief Executive Officer J. Ron Brinson, who has held his post since 1986, the past decade for the Port of New Orleans has been marked by innovation and revitalization. Faced

with growing competition, the port has acted decisively and boldly. In addition to adjusting its wharfage fees to regain a competitive edge, th port has recently completed a majo capital improvement program. As a result, New Orleans can now boas of three new state-of-the-art cargohandling terminals and nearly 3,500 feet of new linear berthing space. Other recent enhancements include the world's largest green coffee processing plant, and new riverfront headquarters. The decade also has brought dramatically increased crui ship activity and the targeting of ne markets around the world. Projects set to be completed include a new trucking approach known as the Clarence Henry Truckway and two new multipurpose cranes on th Mississippi River.

By the end of fiscal year 1988 New Orleans had recaptured the to nage lead among all gulf and South Atlantic ports. The port holds the position as the region's number one importer of finished steel, coffee, and natural rubber. The port's next capital improvement program will provide a new refrigerated cargo facility, expanded facilities for handling general cargo, and increas container handling capacity.

Needless to say, Bienville wouldn't recognize the place, but h would recognize the foresight, imag nation, and hustle that turn great dreams into grand realities.

FROM FAR LEFT TO RIGHT:
NEW ORLEANS IS A PORT OF CALL
FOR BOTH INTERNATIONAL AND RIVER
CRUISES, WITH NEARLY 200,000
PASSENGERS EMBARKING ANNUALLY.

THE PORT OF NEW ORLEANS HEADQUARTERS SHINES IN THE NIGHT.

SOME 2,400 VESSELS DELIVER AND RECEIVE 30 MILLION TONS OF CARGO EACH YEAR AT THE PORT'S 22 MILLION SQUARE FEET OF HANDLING AREAS AND 7.5 MILLION SQUARE FEET OF COVERED STORAGE AREAS.

DONN YOUNG, PORT OF NEW ORLEANS ▼

DONN YOUNG, PORT OF NEW ORLEANS ▼▲

The New Orleans Board of Trade, Ltd.

FOUNDED AS A COMMODITIES EXCHANGE FOR THE LOCAL PRODUCTS AND cargoes that arrived at New Orleans' riverfront, the New Orleans Board of Trade has, over the years, shed some of its early functions. But it still fulfills its most vital mission: Since 1898 it has been the official information link between inbound ships and business interests awaiting their cargoes. ✤ The Board of Trade traces its origin to a chance meeting of five

friends on a wholesale district street corner in the spring of 1880. An impromptu bidding session broke out when one of the men announced that he had pork for sale. These merchants and others began meeting at the same street corner daily for similar transactions until the muggy New Orleans weather inspired them to rent a small room. Since the dignity of an address also demanded the formality of a name, the group dubbed itself the New Orleans Produce Exchange.

The exchange first occupied its present headquarters, a spacious building on Board of Trade Place, in 1883. Attracted by the group's vitality, growing membership, and common purpose, members of the Chamber of Commerce and other business associations became affiliated with the organization. In 1889 the Produce Exchange adopted the name of The New Orleans Board of Trade.

As its influence expanded, the Board of Trade helped spur the creation of a commercial infrastructure that assured New Orleans' position as a leading American port. It has successfully fought for the deepening of passages, the establishment of a Board of Commissioners of the Port of New Orleans to regulate wharves, the creation of the Public Belt Railroad to serve the waterfront, and the routing of the Gulf Intracoastal Waterway from Texas through New Orleans to Florida.

Marine Monitor
On the trading floor of the Board of Trade in those early days, agents displayed samples and sold their commodities hours before the ships actually arrived. Such frenzied and colorful trading activity is now a thing of the past, but it gave rise to

a service that has become vital to the commerce of New Orleans and the entire Mississippi River Valley: the Marine Exchange.

When a vessel enters the mouth of the river, its captain hands over the controls to a bar pilot who guides the ship to the Pilot Town anchorage, at which time a member of the Crescent River Port Pilots Association takes the controls for the remainder of the upriver trip. The pilot maintains telephone contact with the Board of Trade's Marine Exchange personnel, who

issue constant updates of all river and gulf outlet shipping activity to Board of Trade members and subscribers via telephone, fax, and computer modem.

The Board of Trade's other modern activities include compiling shipping statistics for the Port, providing meeting and lounge facilities for its members, and operating a Society of Marine Arbitrators, which is accessible to the legal community. The wonderful old trading room, which sports a magnificent dome that is large enough to contain eight huge murals of local commercial and river scenes, is now available for social functions and business meetings.

Through all its activities, the principal purpose of the Board of Trade remains to serve as a uniting force for the many business interests of New Orleans, whose combined strength can be focused on promoting and maintaining the necessary facilities, services, and freight-rate structure that is essential to the welfare of the city and its port.

VISITORS TO THE NEW ORLEANS BOARD OF TRADE ARE GREETED BY THE BEAUTIFUL WROUGHT IRON GATE OF THE LOGGIA, WHICH FORMS A COVERED ENTRANCEWAY TO THE BUILDING (TOP LEFT).

THE BOARD OF TRADE PLAZA IS FAMOUS FOR ITS CAST IRON SPANISH FOUNTAIN (BOTTOM LEFT).

THE PLAZA ENTRANCE CAN BE ACCESSED FROM MAGAZINE STREET (BOTTOM RIGHT).

Whitney National Bank

KNOWN FOR ITS FAMOUS CLOCKS THAT NOW SPREAD ACROSS THE GULF Coast, the Whitney has been serving its hometown of New Orleans for more than a century. By virtue of being the only New Orleans bank that didn't have to close its doors during the Great Depression, the Whitney can boast of being the city's oldest continuously operating bank. ♣ George Q. Whitney and 11 other original stockholders, including future U.S. Chief

THE WHITNEY CLOCK, A FIXTURE ON MANY WHITNEY BRANCHES, HAS BEEN THE SYMBOL OF THE BANK FOR MORE THAN 70 YEARS.

Justice Edward Douglass White Jr., signed the Articles of Association and received their charter certificate from Washington, D.C., in October of 1883. With James Hayden serving as its first president and White as its first legal counsel, Whitney National Bank opened its doors on November 5, 1883.

THE BUILDING YEARS

In 1888 the Whitney moved into its first permanent home, a landmark on Gravier Street that still serves as the bank's safety deposit department. Located adjacent to the original structure on Gravier, the core of the building—which was built under the presidency of Louisiana sugar baron Charles Godchaux in 1911—sports towering marble columns and acanthus leaf ceiling ornamentation. The 1919 addition of the Common Street Annex provided St. Charles, Gravier, and Common street access to the classic structure.

Early on, the bank earned a reputation as a staunch supporter of local business and civic endeavors. It offered an atmosphere where hometown entrepreneurs could close loans with a handshake and where organizers of local promotions such as the city's first world's fair (the 1884 Cotton Centennial Exposition) could rely on prompt and substantial backing.

The Whitney underwent significant geographic expansion in the early 20th century, acquiring the Germania National Bank in 1905 and six other local banks by 1930. Today, thanks to recent legislative approval of statewide banking, the 1990s have seen the Whitney spread throughout Louisiana to Baton Rouge, Lafayette, Morgan City, Iberia Parish, Covington, Mandeville, and Slidell. The

Whitney has even expanded to Alabama, and a 1996 acquisition in Pensacola made it the first Louisiana bank to enter Florida.

The buildings that were among the bank's early acquisitions—such as the old Pan American Bank building at the corner of Poydras and Camp streets—became the Whitney's first branches. Soon enough, though, the Whitney began building branches from the ground up, beginning with the Margaret Place, Canal Street, Broad Street, and St. Roch Market branches in the mid-1920s.

Since 1972 the bank has maintained a branch in the Cayman Islands to better serve Louisiana's offshore petroleum interests. In the 1990s, while many banks have been closing branches, the Whitney has opened numerous branches in the city and along the coast.

OLD-FASHIONED SERVICE WITH MODERN CONVENIENCE

Support for the New Orleans community is still considered a matter of responsibility and pride

at the Whitney. As proof, the bank established the Cabildo Fund when fire damaged Louisiana's most important landmark in 1988, and supported many economic development, cultural, and educational organizations.

In 1990, when William L. Marks became CEO of the bank, New Orleans and most of the city's financial institutions were struggling under the petroleum industry's collapse and real estate market fluctuations in the 1980s. Since then the turnaround at the Whitney has been dramatic.

While maintaining its tradition of experienced bankers delivering personalized service, the Whitney has anticipated changing customer needs. The Whitney has greatly expanded its consumer banking operations, opening four new branches in New Orleans in 1996, with several more in the planning stages. For consumers who want to "bank around the clock," the Whitney now has more than 90 ATMs, many of which are located at convenience stores, riverboats, and the New Orleans International Airport. The bank also offers 24-hour telephone service and Loan by Phone. A state-of-the-art teller system and wide-area network is being installed in the branches to speed customer service.

Well known for the quality of its commercial account relationship managers, the Whitney has added

new services for commercial customers. The bank has been a leader in international banking services, which are very important in a port city such as New Orleans. It is expanding its operations in Latin and South America and, most recently, throughout the Pacific Rim. The Whitney has also introduced new products for growing businesses, such as special checking accounts, ATM cards, and daily fax reporting. Other new services for commercial customers include employee benefits programs and merchant credit card services.

The Whitney was the first Louisiana bank to expand into Alabama and Florida. This important strategic decision was based on the knowledge that many families and companies do business from Acadiana to the Florida Panhandle. They

can find the Whitney's unique blend of old-fashioned service and modern convenience when they travel across the Gulf South.

Thanks to the Whitney's expert blending of tradition with modern banking concepts and technology, New Orleans' oldest continuously operating bank remains a financial cornerstone of the community today and promises to hold that position in the future.

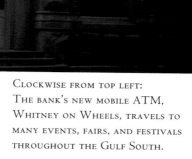

CLOCKWISE FROM TOP LEFT:
THE BANK'S NEW MOBILE ATM, WHITNEY ON WHEELS, TRAVELS TO MANY EVENTS, FAIRS, AND FESTIVALS THROUGHOUT THE GULF SOUTH.

WHITNEY'S GROWING INTERNATIONAL DEPARTMENT IS HEADQUARTERED IN THE BARNES BUILDING, NEXT TO THE MAIN OFFICE. THE BANK RECENTLY RENOVATED THIS HISTORIC BUILDING, WHICH WAS BUILT IN 1884.

A NEW BRANCH ON HIGHWAY 190 IN COVINGTON OPENED IN 1996; THE FIFTH WHITNEY BRANCH IN ST. TAMMANY PARISH.

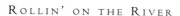

THEIR BEAT IS 250 MILES OF TREACHEROUS MISSISSIPPI RIVER FROM HEAD of Passes to Baton Rouge, and their job is guiding, turning, docking, and towing ships from around the world. They have 18 towboats and two push boats, and they have been "masters of the river" since 1890. ✤ The distinctive red-and-white vessels of Bisso Towboat Company—each with a trademark yellow stripe on its black smokestack—are familiar to anyone who works on or watches the river. The company's line of mighty tugboats performs such tasks as docking and undocking giant tankers and freighters, getting ships back under way that have run aground, assisting disabled ships after collisions or other mishaps, and towing "dead ships" to their outfitting docks.

The long story of the birth, survival, and growth of Bisso Tugboats—a five-generation epic—begins with an adventure tale as daring and captivating as anything from Robert Louis Stevenson or Horatio Alger.

Rafts to Riches
In 1853 ten-year-old Joseph Bissot of Grenoble, France, ran away to sea. Somewhere along the 100-mile Rhone River journey to the Mediterranean, or during his nine-year cabin boy career, he lost the *T* in the Bissot name and found, somewhat by chance, a new home in a new country.

While in New Orleans in 1862, Bisso's ship was seized by Admiral David Farragut's Union blockade, and the crewmen were released to fend for themselves ashore. Bisso found temporary work on Confederate and Union river vessels, and he was employed for a time by an Iberville Parish smithy before signing on for lengthy duty on the Union gunboat *Albatross*, which traveled up the river as far as the Vicksburg area.

By war's end in 1865, Bisso knew the river so well that he was hired to raft logs from Natchez to New Orleans for the Fischer Lumber Company. By 1870 he had gone into the lumber business himself, and in 1890 he bought the tugboat *Joe* and started the towing business at the Walnut Street address in New Orleans where Bisso headquarters remains today.

In 1895 Bisso bought the 500-horsepower tugboat *Leo*, large for that day and age, with his lumber profits—a fateful decision, he realized, when high water and a levee shift suddenly left him with too little property for a lumberyard. Thus Bisso Towboat Company was born, and by the time of Bisso's death in 1907, he owned five tugboats and one river steamer.

Captain Billy
Following Bisso's death, his son Captain William A. Bisso took over the growing business. One year later he opened the New Orleans Coal Company for fueling the coal-burning steamships and smaller vessels on the river. Soon after World War I, the two companies were merged and continued to grow. With strength built on determination and reputation, Bisso was the only tow fleet to survive the Great Depression.

During World War II, Bisso tugboats made a number of daring rescue missions in the Gulf of Mexico to tow ships disabled by enemy submarines into safe waters. World War II also spelled the end

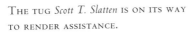

THE TUG *Scott T. Slatten* IS ON ITS WAY TO RENDER ASSISTANCE.

of the hard Depression years, but the company was almost instantly faced with another financially staggering event: the birth of the diesel age. The death of the steam engine meant not only that the Bisso coal operation would quickly vanish, but also that the company faced the cost of converting its own fleet to diesel. As always, the family buckled down and continued to provide the level of service that had made the company famous on the river. Gradually the fleet was converted into the smaller, more agile, and more powerful line of towboats found today.

THIRD AND FOURTH GENERATIONS

When William Bisso died in 1963, his daughter Cecilia Bisso Slatten and grandson Captain William A. Slatten carried on the business. William Slatten, who had been on the river since boyhood, oversaw the final conversion of the fleet to diesel and the expansion of Bisso's role at the Port of New Orleans and along the winding Mississippi River.

Today the Bisso fleet has grown to include 15 twin-screw tugboats, two singles, and one triple, ranging

from 1,800 to 5,200 horsepower; two push boats; a derrick barge; and Bisso's own cargo barges. Major docking facilities are still located at the 800-foot riverfront wharves at the Walnut Street headquarters, but the company has since established a satellite dock and office facility near the Sunshine Bridge in St. James Parish. The company now has 25 anchorages scattered along the Mississippi from Buras to Baton Rouge that provide tie-up facilities for Bisso tugboats awaiting orders along certain stretches of the river. Bisso also offers diversified services, including barge rentals, lineman services, water-barge services, salvage services, and the loading and unloading power of the mighty derrick barge *Thor.*

Clients generally expect an extraordinary desire to please from a towing company that maintains contractual bonds to major steamship lines around the world. Says William Slatten, "It's a family tradition." This translates to a commitment by Bisso Towboat Company to maintain the best personnel, the best attitude, and the best equipment on the Mississippi River.

GERTRUDE GARDNER, REALTORS

A YOUNG VIOLINIST FROM TENNESSEE, GERTRUDE GARDNER GRADUATED FROM THE HARRIMAN CONSERVATORY AND WAS STUDYING COMMERCIAL LAW WHEN HER FATHER MOVED THE FAMILY TO DECATUR, ALABAMA, DURING THE DEPRESSION YEARS. SHE TAUGHT VIOLIN IN DECATUR UNTIL A YOUNG BANKER NAMED WARREN GARDNER MARRIED HER AND WHISKED HER OFF TO HIS NEW FEDERAL LAND BANK JOB IN NEW ORLEANS.

FOUNDER GERTRUDE M. GARDNER

PRESIDENT GLENN M. GARDNER, JR.

THE GARDNER FAMILY INCLUDES (STANDING FROM LEFT) CHIP GARDNER, GAIL GARDNER, DOROTHY WALSH, GLENN GARDNER, (SEATED FROM LEFT) SHARON GARDNER, GERTRUDE GARDNER, WENDY GARDNER, AND CRYSTAL GERTRUDE GARDNER.

▶ PHOTO COURTESY OF THE TIMES-PICAYUNE

Gertrude devoted herself to home and family until her son Glenn entered Tulane and began to excel as a tennis player, becoming the ninth seed nationally in men's singles. This precipitated a need to secure funding for his pursuit of the tournament circuit, which led to Gertrude's decision to enter the real estate profession in order to earn a little extra money.

THE KNACK

Within a year, Gertrude became a leading salesperson for her firm, resigned, and started her own company. Working at first out of the family home, she recruited two friends and eventually her husband as her first associates. Today there are 15 Gertrude Gardner Realtors offices with several hundred sales associates serving eight parishes and two Mississippi Gulf Coast counties. Gertrude herself is still active on the firm's board of directors and with the civic and charitable work of the Gertrude Gardner Foundation. Her company is the oldest major real estate company in the metropolitan area that is still under the same family's leadership. Its slogan "Home grown, locally owned, and nationally known" remains true to this day.

EARLY START

The current president, Glenn M. Gardner Jr., was a licensed agent by age 18. He is a graduate of Loyola University and the Realtors Institute, and is a Certified Real Estate Brokerage Manager, member of The Dozen and Young Presidents Organization, and charter member of the Jefferson Business Council and Real Estate Leaders of America.

With help from Glenn Gardner's leadership, the several family members serving on the board of directors, the excellent staff and sales team, and the continuing inspiration of Gertrude, the company has earned the national PHH

Homequity Five-Star Circle of Excellence Award every year in recent memory. The firm is also ranked in the top 100 real estate companies in the United States and the top 1 percent of all real estate companies nationally!

As a well-known sales leader, Gertrude Gardner, Realtors was one of only six companies selected nationwide by the U.S. government in a pilot program during the recession of the 1980s to handle the sale of the Department of Housing and Urban Development's (HUD's) inventory of Federal Housing Administration (FHA) foreclosure properties. The firm deals in the marketing, sales, leasing, and management of residential, commercial, and industrial properties, and has achieved nearly $500 million in annual sales volume.

Gertrude Gardner Realtors work with premier national relocation networks so newcomers can begin receiving information even before they arrive. The company also maintains its own Internet address (www.gertrude-gardner.com) for worldwide access; an exclusive 24-hour Real Info line, which has interactive real estate information and live operators for booking inspections; and a one-of-a-kind WWL-TV program aired on most Sundays that features film footage and descriptions of available homes.

"This city and region are unique, and each client is special and our market demands excellence," says Gardner. "We're one of a kind—a four-generation family company that is a leading innovator while maintaining its traditional family spirit and personalized service. Our clients appreciate the difference."

New Orleans Museum of Art

The story of the New Orleans Museum of Art, the third oldest fine arts institution in the South, began in 1910 when Isaac Delgado, a local sugar broker and philanthropist, donated $150,000 to build a "temple of art for rich and poor alike." On December 16, 1911, the Museum, a beautiful neo-classic building then known as the Isaac Delgado Museum of Art, presented its first exhibition. ❧ In 1971 the Museum underwent a major expansion, adding the Wisner Education Wing, the Stern Auditorium, and the City Wing, which included the Ella West Freeman Gallery. Recognizing the City of New Orleans' long-term support, the Board of Trustees, in turn, voted to change the name of the institution to the New Orleans Museum of Art.

With the new addition the Museum increased the size and diversity of its collection and attracted international exhibitions such as the *Treasures of Tutankhamen* (1977-1978), *The Search for Alexander* (1982), *The Precious Legacy* (1985), and *Carthage: A Mosaic of Ancient Tunisia* (1988-1989).

In 1993 NOMA completed a major $23 million expansion and renovation project that doubled its size and ranked it among the top 25 percent of museums nationwide. Besides increased space for exhibitions, art storage, library, and educational activities, the expansion also included a new Museum Shop and Courtyard Café.

The added space allowed for a more thorough display of the museum's 45,000 objects and enabled it to attract such blockbuster exhibi-

tions as *Monet: Late Paintings of Giverny form the Musée Marmottan* (1995), *Fabergé in America* (1996-1997), *Andrew Wyeth: The Helga Pictures* (1997), and *Sacred Arts of Haitian Vodou* (1998).

Visitors to the Museum today encounter a comprehensive survey of Western and non-western art from the pre-Christian era to the present. Reflecting the city's cultural heritage, the Museum's collection is particularly strong in French art, including works by such beloved masters as

Monet, Renoir, Gauguin, Degas, Picasso, and others. Objects from the great Mayan culture of Mexico and Central America, works from the Cuzco School in Peru, and Haitian and American painting and sculpture are among the highlights of the Museum's Art of the Americas collection. One of the most popular attractions in the Museum is the special gallery containing three *Imperial Easter Eggs*, the *Imperial Lillies-of-the-Valley Basket*, and numerous other treasures of Peter Carl Fabergé on extended loan from the Matilda Geddings Gray Foundation Collection. The Museum also has nationally recognized collections in sub-Saharan African Art, photography, Japanese painting of the Edo period (1615-1868), and glass works from ancient Egyptian vessels to contemporary glass sculpture. A specially-designed orientation gallery known as *the stARTing point* introduces visitors to the world of art and to the Museum's collection through the use of interactive computers, films, and videos.

CLOCKWISE FROM TOP LEFT:
Roof Tops, Giverny, 1886
CLAUDE MONET
OIL ON CANVAS
ON EXTENDED LOAN FROM THE MRS. FREDERICK M. STAFFORD COLLECTION

NEW ORLEANS MUSEUM OF ART

Archangel with a Matchlock Gun, Salamiel Paxdei (Peace of God)
LATE 17TH CENTURY CIRCLE OF THE MASTER OF CALAMARCA, LAKE TITICACA SCHOOL, BOLIVIA, OIL ON COTTON
MUSEUM PURCHASE

Imperial Napoleonic Easter Egg
PETER CARL FABERGÉ, CREATOR
HENRIK WOGSTROM, WORKMASTER
GOLD, ENAMEL, DIAMONDS, PLATINUM, IVORY, VELVET, SILK
EXTENDED LOAN FROM THE MATILDA GEDDINGS GRAY FOUNDATION COLLECTION

Ⴖew Orleans Limousine Service has occupied a square block at the same Jackson Avenue address since the company's founding in 1941. Circling the block—which is surrounded by a low brick wall broken at regular intervals by a uniform row of small windows—one might be reminded of the old masonry forts that still stand watch over the river, lake, and Barataria Bay approaches to New Orleans. The Jackson Avenue gate leads to a small office building in a large open compound, and the great surrounding wall is a roofed enclosure divided into countless identical bays that once housed the mules and delivery wagons of the old Standard Oil Company. Today it is the garage of the largest limousine service in the Gulf South.

Co-op Caravan

New Orleans Limousine Service was a war child, mothered by necessity during World War II, when the military claimed the production lines of Detroit. Eight leading funeral homes—Tharp-Sontheimer, Schoen, Briede, Leitz-Eagan, Lamana-Panno-Fallo, Laudumiey, McMahon, and Mothe—pooled their Cadillacs, LaSalles, Packards, and other fine cars to create the largest fleet of its day in the nation, used primarily for ambulance and funeral procession purposes on a cooperative basis.

Down through the years the ownership structure of the cooperatively owned company has remained essentially the same, with the addition of the Loewen Group of Canada. The fleet has been expanded and modernized as necessary, and the scope of activities has grown to include corporate, convention, and tour work. In 1957, for instance, New Orleans Limousine Service made the then-largest single purchase of Cadillacs in history, creating for itself the first air-conditioned fleet in the South. Most recently the company purchased 25 new six- and eight-passenger Cadillac Fleetwood limousines, equipped with privacy partitions, spacious leather seating, and state-of-the-art audio systems (also adaptable for cellular telephones, televisions, and beverage bars when requested), for a total fleet of more than 40 pristine and comfortable vehicles.

The fleet's specialty automobiles include Lincoln town cars and motor coaches, the popular new "limousine buses," and various antique vehicles. For weddings or other occasions, the company rolls out the city's finest antique Rolls-Royce. The fleet's "mascot" is a perfectly preserved 1941 Cadillac, a proud reminder of the year New Orleans Limousine Service was founded.

Sleepless Fleet

One might think the company's 3,000-plus funeral processions per year would leave precious little time,

New Orleans Limousine Service's fleet has been expanded and modernized as necessary, and the scope of activities has grown to include corporate and convention work (top).

Several of New Orleans Limousine Service's drivers are licensed tour guides, and it's not unusual for visitors to request cars for leisurely tours of city attractions and River Road plantations (bottom).

anpower, and horsepower for innovation. But Jim Owen, the company's new general manager, is not that one." Since the arrival in 1994 of his CPA and occasional chauffeur, the company has added a new automated accounting system, an energetic new marketing strategy, new concepts in fleet usage, and a 40 percent increase in revenues.

When the Greater New Orleans Tourist and Convention Commission advises its members of major conventions and events that are headed for the city, New Orleans Limousine Service is instantly available by phone or fax to suggest which cars would be suitable for various persons and purposes. For example, a super-stretch limo might be appropriate for head-table guests at a dinner party, while a less conspicuous town car might be appropriate for stars or VIP speakers who prefer not to be spotted by the crowds.

Tours and Tributes

The company's cars have always been available for wedding entourages (about 1,000 a year) and major Carnival krewe requirements during Mardi Gras. In addition, the current volume of airport work is booming, along with the demand for cars and chauffeurs at such diverse activities as proms, concerts, bridal showers, bachelor parties, baby showers, concerts, and ball games, and even the pleasure of spacious limos for bringing mothers and their babies home from the hospital. Several of the company's drivers are licensed tour guides, and it's not unusual for visitors to request cars for leisurely tours of city attractions and River Road plantations. There's even an experimental new program with one hotel in town that allows guests to book their transportation needs automatically upon making their hotel reservations.

New Orleans Limousine Service actually guarantees its punctuality and professionalism as part of its Total Customer Satisfaction Program. For Super Bowls, Sugar Bowls, and exceptionally large conventions, the company simply sends out a call for reinforcements to its affiliates around the state and region.

Chauffeur training in the company's new learning center is thorough and includes actual on-the-job testing. There are regular refreshers on specific events, problem routes and intersections, new hotels, new attractions, and the like.

New Orleans Limousine Service takes pride in its ability to fulfill all its clients' needs, even if it means having a car and chauffeur anywhere in town in 10 or 15 minutes' time. In fact, the biggest advantage of a company with a fleet of this size is its ability to have a clean car and a fresh chauffeur under any circumstances—at the oddest hour of night or the busiest hours of the day, at a month's notice or a moment's notice. Although its fleet has been modernized with the changing times throughout its history, New Orleans Limousine Service's superior level of service will always remain a constant for all its clientele.

Louisiana and New Orleans have a great deal to celebrate, and Magnolia Marketing plays an active role in helping them do just that. For more than half a century Magnolia has been a silent partner in the cultural heritage, and traditions of parades and parties that mark the seasons and significant events of Louisiana life. But like Louisiana life, the story of Magnolia—an affiliate of the Sazerac Company—goes deeper than the parties. Magnolia is also about family.

A Family Affair

Nearly a century ago, in 1898, Newman Goldring was selected for a Schlitz distributorship in the Florida panhandle. There he founded N. Goldring Company, which still can be found today in Pensacola. After Prohibition, Newman and his son Stephen reorganized the company as a wholesale beverage alcohol company, and soon after Newman's retirement, Stephen moved to New Orleans. He and his partner Malcolm Woldenberg, who was then the southern district manager of Seagram, founded a New Orleans-based distributorship of liquors, beers, and fine wines, and named it after Louisiana's state flower.

"Why New Orleans? No question about it," says Stephen's son Bill, a 1964 Tulane business graduate who became executive vice president of Magnolia in 1969, president in 1982, and chairman upon his father's retirement in 1991. "It's because my mother lived in New Orleans. Otherwise we'd still be in Pensacola."

Chairman Bill Goldring, who also heads the philanthropic activities of the Goldring and Woldenberg foundations, joined the company as a warehouseman in 1960 at age 15, then served as driver, salesman, and sales manager on his way to the ranks of upper management. A member of a dozen professional and civic boards and associations—including the Tulane Board of Administrators and Business School Council—he has been generous to his alma mater, providing funding for professorships, buildings, and even a tennis complex, in addition to the cultural, educational, and charitable causes of the community at large.

Bill's son, Jeff, is also a graduate of Tulane University's Business School. After graduation, he apprenticed at Gallo in San Francisco for two years and worked for a year in Atlanta for Georgia Crown Distributing Company. Jeff is now vice president of sales for the parent company.

The company has several divisions and branches including Magnolia-Lafayette, which opened in 1946; Magnolia-Shreveport, which dates back to 1964; Magnolia Marketing Company of Mississippi, which was incorporated in 1970; Crown Beverage of Louisiana, a beer distributor, which opened in 1982; United Beverage of Arizona, which was purchased in 1990; and the New Age Beverage Company, which began operations in New Orleans in 1993.

As chairman emeritus, Stephen Goldring remains active in the business, participating in frequent round-tables with the company's top management. Tom Cole joined the company in Florida and was promoted from vice president of the company's Florida operations to the Magnolia presidency in 1991.

After nearly a century, Magnolia still remains a family-oriented enterprise. Spanning four generations, the family story of Magnolia also extends through the ranks of the company's employees. Today, the company has a staff of 600 in New Orleans alone in addition to 600 other employees who work at operations in other cities across the country. Employees are respected and trusted, and their birthdays, weddings, retirements, and other life events are shared with a familial care and concern that is uncommon in today's corporate world.

Persistence Pays

Today Magnolia Marketing Company is one of the largest privately held businesses in Louisiana. With a dominant share of the beverage market and nearly 20,000 accounts, it is the largest distributor in Louisiana and Arizona and ranks eighth in the nation. It maintains the largest truck fleet and the most warehouse space in the state—a fact that requires the company to use a sophisticated computerized management system. In addition, Magnolia has introduced the concept of refrigerated warehousing for wine storage.

The founding family of Magnolia Marketing Company includes (from left) Vice President Jeffrey Goldring, Founder Stephen Goldring, and Chairman William Goldring.

Magnolia's half-century of step-by-step growth, expansion, and acquisition has largely been the reward of patience. The family members who have run the business had a willingness to purchase small franchises and build them up through competitive pricing, aggressive investment in consumer tastings, heavy point-of-purchase promotions, and retail advertising support.

The company now distributes more than 1,000 brands, including seven of the top 10 brands in the United States. Bacardi is a prime example of Magnolia's brand-development techniques. It was virtually unknown when it was acquired, but is now the number one franchise in Louisiana. Seagram boasts a 12 percent national market share and 28 percent in the Louisiana market.

Many of the brands represented by Magnolia have become household names: Taaka, Seagram, Bacardi, Smirnoff, José Cuervo, and Wild Turkey. In addition to an extensive spirit portfolio, the company is one of the largest distributors in the United States of fine wines including such recognizable names as Robert Mondavi, Kendall-Jackson, Sebastiani, Gallo, and Paul Masson. The company also handles other nonalcoholic beverage products such as Evian, Snapple, and A & W.

Magnolia's products are enjoyed by people all over the region, from Bourbon Street and Mardi Gras parade routes to New Orleans' incomparable restaurants. Although most people who enjoy fine spirits are unaware of the distribution process that brings their favorite beverages to them, the Magnolia family is committed to ensuring that they will never have cause for concern. The company is accustomed, after all, to being the silent partner in celebrations.

TOP: MAGNOLIA MARKETING COMPANY'S CORPORATE OFFICERS INCLUDE (FROM LEFT) AL JANUSA, TOM COLE, PAUL FINE, AND CLYDE GIESENSCHLAG.

BOTTOM: MAGNOLIA IS THE LARGEST DISTRIBUTOR IN LOUISIANA AND RANKS EIGHTH IN THE NATION. CONSEQUENTLY, THE COMPANY MAINTAINS THE LARGEST TRUCK FLEET AND THE MOST WAREHOUSE SPACE IN THE STATE.

ODAY'S BURKS-FARBER CLINICS AND KENNER OUTPATIENT SURGICAL Center are the results of pioneering advances in dermatology made by Dr. James Willis Burks III and the enthusiasm and farsightedness of his colleague Dr. George A. Farber. Offering total skin care from cosmetology to dermatology—including the diagnosis, treatment, and surgical services of specialists in the field—the clinics are equipped to handle any procedure

GEORGE A. FARBER, M.D., IS THE MEDICAL DIRECTOR OF THE BURKS-FARBER CLINICS.

without referral and on a cost-effective outpatient basis.

Burks was only 33 years old when he became the first dermatologist at Ochsner Clinic, and at age 34 he founded his own clinic: Burks Dermatology Clinic. As his own explorations in the field of dermatology flourished—extending finally into the long-awaited arena of dermatological surgery—Burks became more and more committed to teaching his specialty at Tulane Medical School.

Burks taught until 1970, when he entrusted his teaching responsibilities to his protégé, Farber. In 1972 the two men became founding members of the American Society for Dermatologic Surgery, for which Farber has served 10 years either as director or as an officer. Farber received the Service Award for Special Contribution in 1995. The American Academy of Aesthetic and Restorative Surgery is a new society he cofounded in 1991 and on which he serves as an officer and director. Farber is also a retired Air Force officer and served in Vietnam, for which he received the Bronze Star among other medals. Farber also continues to devote a significant amount of his time to teaching.

EXPANSION YEARS

In 1974, after years of expanding the practice, the partners moved the clinic into the Elk Place Medical Plaza where it remained until Burks' death in 1978. In 1985 the Burks Dermatology, Allergy, and Dermatological Surgery Clinic opened in Place St. Charles. Today the Burks-Farber Clinics include the Kenner Dermatology Clinic and Kenner Outpatient Surgical Center in the Professional Building at Kenner Regional Medical Center, the Terrytown Allergy and

Dermatology Clinic, the Chalmette Dermatology Clinic, the Hammond Dermatology and Dermatologic Surgery Clinic, the Picayune Dermatology Clinic, the Slidell Dermatology Clinic, and the Covington Dermatology Clinic.

Farber's Gulf South Medical and Surgical Institute, also located in the Kenner hospital complex's Professional Building, provides postgraduate training for board-certified and board-eligible dermatologists in a one-year fellowship program. Accredited in 1985, it is one of only a half-dozen such programs worldwide.

EXPERTS

The 10-member team of dermatologists and dermatologic surgeons at Burks-Farber includes recognized experts in aesthetic and restorative surgery, and Dr. John Louis Ratz, a world authority on laser surgery and

a master of the new Mohs micrographic surgical technique.

For the purpose of professional cosmetic counseling, which is especially important in some pre- and postsurgical settings, every Burks-Farber Clinic provides studio analysis and treatment by Letti Lynn, an internationally known beauty expert and aesthetics instructor. She is the international president of the Aestheticians International Association, as well as a cosmetologist, microdermapigmentologist, and skin care specialist.

The history of Burks-Farber Clinics and of dermatology in the Gulf South are one and the same. The practice founded by two leaders in the field has become a unique gathering place for the sharing of knowledge and facilities among dedicated experts in the diagnosis and treatment of every skin-related condition known to medical science.

MARKS PAPER COMPANY

THE OFFICE WALLS OF MARKS PAPER COMPANY FEATURE BACKLIT DISPLAYS OF watermarks dating to 1710. The entranceway is a museum of vintage paper-production instruments, including a Mullen tester for gauging bursting strength and a tearing register, both of which were already antiques when Sam A. Marks founded the company nearly 50 years ago. Impressive for its decor, Marks Paper Company has also earned the respect of the entire printing community.

Making its business debut in 1948, Marks Paper was a small "cut-size" paper company that was capitalized with $1,800 and a Studebaker. In 1968 the company was still listed as the smallest paper company in New Orleans, but by the mid-1970s it was a large multipurpose paper supplier that centered on the needs of the local design and printing community. Today, nearly half a century after opening its doors, Marks Paper ranks as the oldest family-owned paper distributorship in Louisiana and as the largest in southeast Louisiana and along the I-55 corridor as far north as Jackson, Mississippi.

COMMITTED TO QUALITY

The transition from office paper purveyor to major printing supplier is due to a commitment to quality. As clients choose from an assortment of in-stock coated paper and specialty papers, they are assisted by skilled professionals who are specially trained to analyze and recommend certain papers for specific needs. The team recently earned the Williamhouse Merchant of the Year Award.

"Quality Papers, Quality People" is both a slogan and a guiding principle for Marks Paper. To that end, the full-service company utilizes such resources as SCRIPTURA, a computer program developed by Vice President Allen Marks, which puts the company's inventory at the designers' fingertips. Another program, SPEC-CHECK, created by President Alan Rosenbloom, assists managers at Marks in tracking orders and quotes as they crisscross among graphic designers and printers, and assures customers of the lowest price with no possibility of quote error. Marks Paper's unique Design Library/Resource Center houses 12.5-by-19-inch sample sheets in all colors, weights, and finishes of every line Marks has in stock or can order, including 40 grades of recycled papers. The center also features samples of the various printing techniques and has Louisiana's only Annual Report Library, where hundreds of innovative annual reports can be inspected by designers. In addition, the company offers an in-house School of Paper Knowledge for beginning and intermediate sales and design professionals who seek a basic understanding of papermaking and selection.

Both Rosenbloom and Marks feel a strong responsibility to the community that has made their enterprise a success, energetically supporting the United Way and nearly 200 other nonprofit organizations in the city. Rosenbloom serves on the boards of nine civic and charitable organizations, and Marks was the president of the New Orleans SPCA and served on the advisory committee of the Young Executives Forum of the National Paper Trade Association.

Experience, innovation, reliability, and true concern for the well-being of clients and community are all factors that set this great family business apart from huge and faceless national distributorships.

LEFT: THE STAFF AT MARKS PAPER COMPANY INCLUDES (FROM LEFT) CUSTOMER SERVICE MANAGER DAWN SALISBURY, CHIEF FINANCIAL OFFICER VICKI BOUDREAU, ASSISTANT WAREHOUSE MANAGER KENNETH SINGLETON, PRESIDENT ALAN ROSENBLOOM, CHAIRMAN OF THE BOARD SAM MARKS, VICE PRESIDENT ALLEN MARKS, MANAGEMENT INFORMATION SYSTEMS COORDINATOR KAY LISOTTA, WAREHOUSE MANAGER DONALD RHODES, AND PURCHASING AGENT SUSIE ESTEVES.

BELOW: THE COMPANY'S PRINCIPALS INCLUDE (FROM LEFT) VICE PRESIDENT ALLEN MARKS, CHIEF FINANCIAL OFFICER VICKI BOUDREAU, CHAIRMAN OF THE BOARD SAM MARKS AND PRESIDENT ALAN ROSENBLOOM.

M.G. Maher & Company, Inc.

I N 1949 AT THE PORT OF NEW ORLEANS, A NEW FLEDGLING IMPORT/EXPORT brokerage and forwarding business spread its wings. Under the direction of Morris G. Maher, the new organization consisted of only three people—two licensed customs brokers and one employee. But even in its infancy, M.G. Maher & Company was dedicated to the efficient, safe, and economical movement of goods in both domestic and international trade.

Today the employees and associates of the time-tested company form a global network, and M.G. Maher has become one of the largest and most diverse full-service logistic management companies in the nation. Its staff have become intimately familiar with the technical details, laws, personalities, systems, routines, and quirks associated with shipping—including the tracing of inland movement to seaboard; booking of advance and timely cargo space; rate negotiation; warehousing as required at U.S. ports or inland destinations; all documentation, banking, and intermodal transportation; truck and project management; marine and transportation insurance; customs consulting; computer reports per clients' requirements; auditing; and freight payment systems. In short, M.G. Maher provides a full range of logistics management services to its customers.

The company has also created a contract division called Maherbarge for service throughout the Gulf Coast and the entire Mississippi River system, offering competitive rates for barging, single origin-to-destination quotes, just-in-time door delivery, and high-tech dispatch reports.

ACROSS THE COUNTRY AND AROUND THE WORLD

Upon Morris Maher's death in 1973, his wife, Paula L. Maher, took the helm. M.G. Maher still remains a family business, as Paula Maher steers the operation with strong counsel and assistance from other members of the Maher family as well as from a staff of experienced and dedicated professionals, many of whom have been with the company since the beginning.

In 1976 M.G. Maher experienced a breakthrough as computerization of its import system for the clearance of cargo eliminated time-consuming typing, handwritten entries, and traffic orders.

At the same time, its capability to handle export documentation on its computer kept pace with its expanding import system.

In 1980 M.G. Maher & Company, Inc. received its Interstate Commerce Commission permit, which added another dimension of brokering domestic transportation to its growing full-service capabilities.

It also established an Automated Broker Interface. In fact, the Automated Broker Interface Award was bestowed on M.G. Maher on May 1, 1987, by the Commissioner of Customs to recognize the company's industry leadership as the first firm in the nation to interface with the U. S. Customs Service.

The long-standing position of trust and respect that M.G. Maher shares with ocean and domestic carriers, banks, insurance companies, and other service providers enables it to structure the optimum combination of price and service levels that allow customers to concentrate their resources on their core activities. The company performs a broad range of logistics services that are essential to the customer-supplier relationships among companies. These services are provided for deliveries made throughout the United States and to or from any other country in the world through a package that is consistent in price and level of performance.

NATIONAL COMPUTER HOOKUPS

The transportation and management of cargo have become a more complex and demanding business in the multimodal electronic age.

ALTHOUGH M.G. MAHER HAS ALWAYS LED THE INDUSTRY IN THE DEVELOPMENT AND ASSIMILATION OF NEW SYSTEMS AND CAPABILITIES, THE ORIGINAL IDEAS HELD BY MORRIS G. MAHER REMAIN AND WILL CONTINUE TO BE HIS COMPANY'S OPERATING PHILOSOPHY. M.G. MAHER'S STAFF HAVE BECOME INTIMATELY FAMILIAR WITH THE TECHNICAL DETAILS, LAWS, PERSONALITIES, SYSTEMS, ROUTINES, AND QUIRKS ASSOCIATED WITH SHIPPING.

OSCAR RAJO

Although headquartered in New Orleans, the company—with a staff of more than 125 employees throughout their offices—makes it their daily business to stay one step ahead of these constantly changing requirements. Their computer interfaces with shippers and their suppliers, plants, warehouses, terminal locations, U.S. Customs, U.S. Department of Commerce, and ocean and air carriers.

M.G. Maher provides a host of services to clients on a regular basis, including warehousing as required at U.S. ports or inland destinations, booking cargo, banking, documentation, cargo insurance, delivery of cargo to dock, ship chartering, and carrier selection.

Additional services provided include barge, rail, or truck transportation; customs consulting; air transportation; rate negotiation; auditing; freight payment systems; and computer reports relating to client requirements.

No-Loss Assurance

Computers come and go, but nothing replaces the value of one-on-one personal service and concern for each individual client. Maher is not a faceless corporation. Although M.G. Maher has always led the industry in the development and assimilation of new systems and capabilities, the original ideas held by Morris G. Maher remain and will continue to be his company's operating philosophy.

Internally, the organization Maher created is guided by the principles of total quality management, which defines the standards of inter-

▲▼ OSCAR RAJO

▼ OSCAR RAJO

relationships within the company and with its 1,500-plus trade clients as well. The self-imposed standard of performance that the founder branded on the consciousness of every company representative, both at home and abroad, remains M.G. Maher's obligation and inspiration to this very day: "We are a service business and, as such, we offer no delays, no excuses."

1950-1996

1956 CENTURY GRAPHICS CORPORATION	1958 UNIVERSITY OF NEW ORLEANS	1969 ROYAL SONESTA HOTEL AND CHATEAU SONESTA HOTEL	1974 MONTGOMERY, STIRE & PARTNERS
1956 L&L OIL COMPANY	1965 DIXIE WEB GRAPHIC CORPORATION	1972 NEW ORLEANS MARRIOTT	1976 SIGMA COATINGS
1957 WWL-TV, CHANNEL 4	1968 WASTE MANAGEMENT OF NEW ORLEANS	1973 DOUBLETREE • HOTEL NEW ORLEANS	1977 EYE SURGERY CENTER OF LOUISIANA

CENTURY GRAPHICS CORPORATION

N 1956 FOUNDERS CARL AND GERARD EBERTS COULD NOT HAVE DREAMED OF Century Graphics today. The little one-press commercial printing company they founded on Magazine Street has mushroomed into a giant national company. The Metairie operation houses presses 50 yards long that produce 20 miles of super-wide full-color printed materials each hour. The plant creates advertising supplements distributed in practically every

newspaper in the Mid-South. That's 700 million retail advertising inserts per year, each one of which can be up to 64 pages in length.

Each night, trains and trucks deliver massive rolls of paper—22,500 tons each year for the New Orleans plant alone—to be transformed into truckloads of retail advertising inserts for the following week's newspapers.

And that's just the local picture. Nationally, Century Graphics also creates inserts at printing plants in Hartford, Connecticut; Omaha, Nebraska; and Winchester, Virginia, where a company-wide total of 15 giant presses produce 3.2 billion inserts a year.

"Our greatest growth has been in the past 10 years," says President and CEO Michael D. Moffitt, who, with an investment group, purchased Century Graphics in 1994. "We plan to double our size again in the next three to five years, in terms of sales and press capacity."

SPECIALIZING SPELLS SUCCESS

Inserts, which Moffitt calls an "in-your-face advertising medium," have enjoyed a phenomenal boom in popularity over the past 15 years. And the growth and success of

Century Graphics is tied directly to its decision to specialize in newspaper advertising inserts. Century's mission emphasizes its total focus on the retail advertising business: "To provide exceptional quality, innovation, service, and value, assuring our customers effective advertising circular programs. We are focused on the principle that consistent superior service to customers is the foundation for employment security, profits, and return on investment."

Moffitt, who brings 22 years of printing expertise to Century Graphics, is a champion of the benefits of technology in the world of printing. "We're committed to versatility and flexibility when it comes to meeting our customers' needs," says Moffitt, who is a member of the board of directors of the Graphic Arts Technical Foundation and holds patents in image processing and data-compression technology. "That requires us to have every technological advantage at our fingertips. Our computerization and state-of-the-art

presses have actually slashed the cost of full-color printing for our clients, not to mention shortening the lead time needed for vital last-minute changes in their advertising messages."

It was Century Graphics, in fact, that pioneered the use of "heat set" printing for advertising supplements, a technique that introduced the ultrasharp smudge-free printing and high-quality coated papers that set the standard for today's inserts.

PEOPLE-POWERED

Moffitt believes it is the people, not the machinery, of Century Graphics that allow the company to succeed in its mission to provide exceptional quality, innovation, service, and value to its customers across the country. "Our press crews," he says, "are integral teams of top craftsmen—trained and cross-trained—who continue to build their own skills and to help train newcomers as the company grows. Pride is high, skills and experience are deep, and these teams are truly the lifeblood of Century Graphics."

NEAR RIGHT: CENTURY GRAPHICS' METAIRIE HEADQUARTERS

FAR RIGHT: THE METAIRIE DIVISION TOP CREW OF 1995 INCLUDES (FROM LEFT) BRUCE LEBLANC; DAVE CARAWAY, VICE PRESIDENT AND GENERAL MANAGER, METAIRIE DIVISION; JOHNELL WADE; JOHN THOMAS; WILLIE CHEATHAM; EDUARDO JUAREZ; FREDDIE LOPEZ, SHIFT SUPERVISOR; AND ALVARO MORA, PRESSROOM MANAGER.

L & L Oil Company

FORTY YEARS OF SUCCESS AND JUST BEGINNING" WAS THE PROUD SLOGAN that greeted L&L Oil Company employees and customers in the company's anniversary year of 1996. But it's the tried-and-true motto that appears on the headquarters door—"Fueled with Enthusiasm and Pumped Up with Pride"— that truly portrays the chutzpah of the marine service company that has experienced tremendous growth since its founding in the uncertain days of

the mid-20th century. The company began in 1956 when Leon Levy and Lee Adams, who between them owned one boat and one barge, combined their assets and their first initials to create the L&L fuel delivery service for oil producers who drilled in the inland and off-shore waters of southeast Louisiana.

THE WAR FOR INDEPENDENTS

Only the largest oil companies were in the gulf in those days, and because each demanded its own company's fuel and lubricants, suppliers were limited in the number of support fleets they could service. Levy and Adams, however, delivered to one of the largest operators—Texaco. The partners plowed every dollar of profits into building up their small fleet, thereby finding them-selves in a good position to compete in the 1970s, when the infamous oil embargo created a fever pitch of gulf-drilling activities by dozens of new independent drillers. The independents weren't particular about brand names, and they became fair game for any fuel supplier with enough ambition and dependability to get their business. L&L came out on top, and has stayed there ever since.

In the 1970s new profits allowed L&L's flotilla to extend service to the barge-based rigs of Louisiana's inland drilling activity. This action unfortunately left L&L's new owner, Leon's son Frank, holding the bag when many of his boats were idled by the oil-price collapse of the 1980s. Rather than mothballing the fleet, however, L&L stationed craft and crews along the Louisiana coast to service the offshore drilling industry. With the purchase of Berwick Bay Oil

Company, by the end of the decade L&L had established a dozen fuel supply points between the Mississippi River and Sabine Pass, Texas. L&L had also set up full-service midstream fueling operations in the Port of New Orleans and in Port Arthur, Texas.

L&L's bold maneuvering in the face of possible disaster again left it poised to be a full participant in the growing rebound of Louisiana oil exploration in the late 1990s. Today the company is the largest supplier of diesel fuel and lubricants to the offshore drilling industry. And its newest subsidiary, L&L Environmental Service, is a competitor to be reckoned with in spill recovery, emergency response, and oil-and-filter recycling.

A LOOK AHEAD

Continued expansion through strategic acquisitions lies in L&L's future, but its present growth is taking the form of an increasing variety of services offered at the company's existing facilities. "We're proud of our

WITH LOCATIONS IN MORGAN CITY (LEFT AND BELOW) AND ELSEWHERE THROUGHOUT LOUISIANA AND TEXAS, L&L OIL COMPANY IS "FUELED WITH ENTHUSIASM AND PUMPED WITH PRIDE." HEADQUARTERED IN METAIRIE, THE COMPANY IS THE LARGEST SUPPLIER OF DIESEL FUEL AND LUBRICANTS TO THE OFFSHORE DRILLING INDUSTRY.

survival and growth in this volatile and cyclical industry," says President Frank L. Levy. "We're proud of our customer list that includes the greatest companies in the world and in our own region. And we're extremely proud of the 275 men and women of L&L whose efforts help us keep our pledge to meet or exceed our customers' requirements."

ENTLE SWELLS OF WATER LAPPING THE LOWER STEPS OF THE Pontchartrain seawall, bushels of red-ripe Creole tomatoes in the yellowing light of dawn, the Canal Street ferry pushing across the current toward its west bank landing—these are a few quiet moments in time that many New Orleanians are unable to experience firsthand due to the hustle and bustle of everyday life. Understanding this, WWL-TV, Channel 4

uses the television screen to drop such glimpses of New Orleans beauty into its viewers' lives between segments of some of the best local news coverage in the nation.

The call letters WWL have been associated with innovative broadcasting since 1922, when Channel 4's radio ancestor was born. The station's initial broadcast reached area residents when the Gulf South's first AM radio signal was transmitted from a physics laboratory at Loyola University. WWL joined the Columbia Broadcasting System in 1935, and WWL-TV has been a CBS affiliate since it went on the air in 1957.

Familiar Faces

WWL-TV finds strength in continuity, which extends from its network affiliation to its habit of attracting and keeping top professionals. One such person is General Manager J. Michael Early, who has been the foundation of the station's success for more than 35 of its 40 years of history. The same is true of on-camera personnel—such as 36-year editorialist Phil Johnson and 30-year investigative reporter and longtime anchor Bill Elder—all

of whom have won the trust and admiration of the station's viewing audience.

In addition, veteran Co-anchor Angela Hill may have the most recognized face in New Orleans, while newcomer Hoda Kotb has been voted best female anchor more than once in local surveys. Another recent addition, Co-anchor/Reporter Dennis Woltering, has been widely praised within the community for his in-depth reporting and political insights.

Many viewers depend on the station's *Eyewitness Morning News* with Eric Paulsen and Sally-Ann Roberts, sports coverage by veteran Anchor/

Reporter/Analyst Jim Henderson, and "satisfaction" from Action/ ConsumerWatch reporter Bill Capo. With double-digit years of service in the weather department, Dave Barnes and Don Westbrook command great trust and respect. And Nash Roberts, an institution unto himself, still comes out of retirement to serve as hurricane consultant when the big storms get too close for comfort.

WWL-TV also has a number of specialists, such as *Morning Show* chef and "Naturally N'Awlins" observation man Frank Davis, as well as local television colorist Ronnie Virgets—both of whom have delightful dialects and localisms that

prime-time public forums and political debates continue to involve audiences in the issues of the day.

WWL-TV was also the first to combine its energies with cable accessibility in order to create its own around-the-clock news service. These *NewsWatch* editions on Channel 15 are first aired live and then repeated every half-hour until the next live broadcast. Today this 24-hour "news on demand" concept has been imitated in many major markets.

Since its first broadcast through radio signals more than 70 years ago, WWL has never ceased to serve the New Orleans community. Bringing its viewing public an endless string of firsts, the station has been a broadcasting leader not only to its local audience, but among its national peers as well. With its rich history, cutting-edge programming, and staff of seasoned professionals, WWL-TV will continue to expand the frontier of the possibilities that television has to offer.

CLOCKWISE FROM TOP LEFT: WWL-TV'S FRENCH QUARTER COURTYARD PROVIDES AN INTERVIEW SETTING FOR ANCHOR/REPORTER SALLY-ANN ROBERTS.

THERE'S ALWAYS SOMETHING GOOD *In the Kitchen* WITH RESIDENT CHEF FRANK DAVIS.

THE NATION'S LONGEST-RUNNING TELEVISION EDITORIALIST IS NEW ORLEANS' OWN PHIL JOHNSON.

call to mind certain earlier personalities: Dizzy Dean, Will Rogers, and Hap Glaudi. When Carnival time comes around, special reporter Arthur "Mr. Mardi Gras" Hardy presents his "Eye on Carnival" reports throughout the season. On Mardi Gras day, he is accompanied by nearly a dozen Channel 4 personalities through broadcasts from five key camera locations around the Greater New Orleans area.

In addition to programs that feature the station's personalities, human interest features, and each day's top stories, WWL-TV offers two series that are designed to instill pride, pleasure, and community identity. Channel 4's *Spirit of Louisiana* music videos have won the station an Emmy Award for capturing New Orleans' wide variety of regional music, while *Louisiana Made, Louisiana Proud* has brought recognition of local ingenuity and energy in business and industry.

FIRSTS AND BESTS

In almost every television market in America, there is fierce competition for ratings, but in New Orleans it's no contest. WWL-TV's *Eyewitness News* commands more viewers than the combined totals of the competition, assuring the station a top spot in the national rankings of local network affiliates. For example, WWL-TV has won the National Edward R. Murrow Award—which is given to the country's best overall news operation—twice in the past 10 years. Perhaps even more impressive are the station's five George Foster Peabody Awards, most recently won for veteran anchorman Bill Elder's 31-part series on local drug rehabilitation fraud titled "Facing Reality: Politics, Drugs, and Waste."

Channel 4's commitment to community journalism has driven it to produce more than 26 hours of news programming every week. In fact, the station led the market with five news slots daily, even before adding its 5:30 a.m. edition. WWL-TV was the first station in the country with a two-hour morning news program, which is still one of the nation's top-rated morning news shows. The station's frequent

O N September 5, 1958, the University of New Orleans (UNO) opened its doors for the first time to 1,500 freshman students. Back then the university's "doors" belonged to converted military barracks and buildings of an abandoned naval air station overlooking Lake Pontchartrain. ✦ Today UNO annually enrolls 16,000 students in more than 100 degree programs at both the undergraduate and graduate levels. UNO's doors now

open to classrooms and research facilities that mark a modern comprehensive university. In fact the university's original 195-acre campus has grown to nearly 350 acres on the lakefront in addition to several satellite locations in the New Orleans metropolitan area.

In fewer than four decades the University of New Orleans has dis-

tinguished itself in scholarship, research, and community service. Most recently UNO has been elected to the National Association of State Universities and Land-Grant Colleges (NASULGC), the nation's oldest public higher education association; the Association of American Colleges, a group of major U.S. colleges committed to improving undergraduate liberal arts education; and Urban 13, an organization of urban universities considered the best in the nation.

UNO has forged public and private partnerships that keep it on the leading edge of issues that impact both the local and global community, ranging from national defense and environmental research to the visual arts. Some of the most recent partnerships include UNO's Gulf Coast Region Marine Technology Center, which participates in MARITECH, a national program to improve the international competitiveness of the U.S. shipbuilding industry; the UNO-Audubon Institute Affiliation, an innovative program in conservation biology that destines New Orleans to become a major center in the study of endangered species; UNO at John C. Stennis Space Center, a program that assists NASA in training top scientists and engi-

neers for the national space effort; the UNO Business-Higher Education Council, an alliance between the business community and higher education committed to economic development; the Roger H. Ogden Museum of Southern Art and the National D-Day Museum, both part of the UNO-Lee Circle Center for the Arts that promises to revitalize New Orleans' historic Lee Circle and Warehouse Arts District; the UNO Technology Enterprise Center (UNO/TEC) that, with its business incubator and Small Business Development Center, is expected to generate an annual economic impact of $25 million in new spending; and the Center for Energy Resources Management (CERM), a collaborative initiative of federal, state, and private supporters that focuses research on energy sources, conservation, and the environment. CERM and the Louisiana Public Health Laboratories will be the anchor tenants of UNO's 56-acre Research and Technology Park.

UNO is a member of the Louisiana State University system and was originally established as Louisiana State University in New Orleans (LSUNO). In 1974 the university was granted its name change, indicating the strong linkage of the university's mission, character, and destiny to the community it serves.

Since its founding, UNO has granted over 40,000 degrees. Amazingly, 80 percent of UNO alumni stay to live and work in Louisiana and the New Orleans area. As it prepares to enter the 21st century, the University of New Orleans remains dedicated to the educational, economic, and social initiatives that have meshed its goals with those of the people of New Orleans and Louisiana.

Dixie Web Graphic Corporation

ONG BEFORE NEW ORLEANS' WAREHOUSE DISTRICT WAS TRANSFORMED into posh surroundings, an ancient warehouse on Annunciation Street became the home of Dixie Web Graphic Corporation, the premier cold-web-offset printing company of southeast Louisiana. The company was actually born in smaller quarters nearby when young Ralph B. Hay and two associates acquired a contract to produce the *Clarion Herald*, the

120,000-circulation newspaper of the Diocese of New Orleans. But rapid growth soon led the young company to move to the spacious warehouse facility it now occupies.

Although Ralph Hay was born in Ohio, he moved to the South as a boy when his father became circulation manager of the *New Orleans Item*. There he met his wife, Josie, at Tulane University and Newcomb College in the 1960s. Josie not only became his partner in marriage, but also began helping the company as the need arose with tasks in accounting, the art department, the mail room, and computer programming.

Over its long history, Dixie Web has earned an enviable reputation for its ability to produce high-quality publications with an emphasis on customer service, dependability, technical expertise, and quick turnaround time. Thanks to the variety of business needs it serves, the company has mastered a wide range of publications from newspapers and advertising tabloids to magazines, catalogs, newsletters, and circulars.

If Dixie Web can be said to have a particular specialty, it would be producing daily convention newspapers. New Orleans is blessed with an endless parade of gatherings, and Dixie Web has provided its publishing services to many such events over the years. The company was even chosen by the 1988 Republican National Convention to publish its daily newspaper.

FULL-SERVICE CAPABILITIES

Dixie Web is a full-service printing company, where products can be taken from concept to publication using state-of-the-art technical

resources every step of the way. Services include art, computer design, and typography; publication and publishing consulting; cold-web-offset printing; bindery for customized publications; and customized mailing services and delivery.

"With the new computer technology now available to companies, it's no longer necessary to have near access to a printing company," says Josie, citing publications as far away as California, Nevada, New Mexico, Texas, and Georgia that use Dixie Web's services. "We have an aggressive sales and marketing department that complements our excellent technical and production capabilities. We're poised for further growth without compromising our commitment to excellent service and high-quality publications."

With 18 units of Harris presses, two saddle-stitching machines, a folder, two mailing machines, computerized production processes, and 60 highly skilled employees, Dixie Web produces 6 million impressions per month. Recently the company installed a six-unit line with capabili-

ties for square tabloids as well as gatefold circulars.

Although Ralph Hay died in the spring of 1993, his legacy of integrity, honesty, and professionalism is carried on by his wife and business partner. Much like Josie—who many customers fondly remember as one who would roll up her sleeves and help in any department—Dixie Web has earned client confidence.

"Perhaps the greatest testimonial to Dixie Web's premier reputation in this industry," Josie says, "is the large number of customers who have been with us so long, some as many as 30 years. Everyone here works hard on every job to maintain that enviable relationship with every customer."

CLOCKWISE FROM TOP LEFT: FOUNDER RALPH HAY'S LEGACY OF INTEGRITY, HONESTY, AND PROFESSIONALISM IS CARRIED ON BY HIS WIFE AND BUSINESS PARTNER, JOSIE, WHO PLANS TO CONTINUE DIXIE WEB'S GROWTH WITHOUT COMPROMISING ITS COMMITMENT TO EXCELLENT SERVICE AND HIGH-QUALITY PUBLICATIONS.

DIXIE WEB IS A FULL-SERVICE PRINTING COMPANY, WHERE PRODUCTS CAN BE TAKEN FROM CONCEPT TO PUBLICATION USING STATE-OF-THE-ART TECHNICAL RESOURCES EVERY STEP OF THE WAY.

IF DIXIE WEB CAN BE SAID TO HAVE A PARTICULAR SPECIALTY, IT WOULD BE PRODUCING DAILY CONVENTION NEWSPAPERS.

ITH A LITTLE HELP FROM WASTE MANAGEMENT OF NEW ORLEANS, THE City of New Orleans became one of the first municipalities in the country to apply the concepts of privatization and public-private partnership to its residents' solid waste needs. As the city's largest solid waste services company, Waste Management was one of the first such companies to approach city government about the privatization/partnership concept,

A STATE-OF-THE ART TRANSFER STATION, OWNED BY THE CITY OF NEW ORLEANS AND OPERATED BY WASTE MANAGEMENT OF NEW ORLEANS, IS ONE PART OF THE TRANSPORTATION SYSTEM THAT PROVIDES FOR THE TRANSFER OF THE CITY'S ALMOST 1,400 TONS PER DAY OF RESIDENTIAL AND COMMERCIAL SOLID WASTE TO PECAN GROVE, WASTE MANAGEMENT'S SUBTITLE D LANDFILL IN MISSISSIPPI (RIGHT).

RESIDENTS IN SELECTED CITIES AND PARISHES THROUGHOUT THE METRO AREA ARE ENJOYING THE RECENTLY INTRODUCED AUTOMATED COLLECTION SYSTEM. THE 96-GALLON CARTS ARE GRABBED BY A ROBOTIC ARM ON THE COLLECTION VEHICLE, DUMPED INTO THE BIN, AND REPLACED ON THE CURB. THE DRIVER CONTROLS THE ENTIRE OPERATION FROM THE VEHICLE'S CAB (BELOW).

and began servicing the Algiers section of the city in 1977.

The present New Orleans division was founded locally in 1968 as American Waste and Pollution Control. In 1972 the company was purchased by Waste Management, Inc. of Oak Brook, Illinois. Today the parent company, WMX Technologies, Inc. with annual revenues of $10.2 billion, is known in the industry as the world's largest provider of solid waste and environmental services.

Southeast Louisiana

Waste Management of New Orleans operates as a cooperative effort between its residential and commercial collection fleets and facilities and its pickup station and landfill management team. With almost 300 employees among the various divisions, the company provides a $73 million

◀ BURTON STEEL

annual economic impact for the city and well over $100 million annual economic impact for the six-parish metropolitan area.

The residential division's most recent innovation is the introduction of fully automated collection to selected parishes and cities in the metro area. This service utilizes 96-gallon carts that are lifted and dumped robotically into collection vehicles. For both commercial and residential use statewide, the company has introduced material recycling facilities (MRFs) and transfer facilities, where solid waste vehicles deposit their loads into giant 18-wheelers for shipment to such sites as Pecan Grove, Waste Management's Subtitle D landfill in Mississippi.

Waste Management of New Orleans' commercial division began providing services to businesses and industries in 1968 as the former

American Waste & Pollution Control. For more than two decades, major businesses, such as Shell Oil Company, Union Carbide, Lockheed-Martin, Cytec Industries, and Amax Nickel, have relied on Waste Management to provide waste handling and disposal, as well as other related environmental services.

From large industries to small businesses, service is a key ingredient of Waste Management's success in the Crescent City. Leading businesses and organizations rely on Waste Management's commercial operation for their day-to-day projects and, in conjunction with Waste Management's residential division, for the numerous special events held in the New Orleans area. Services such as front-loading dumpsters and roll-off industrial waste containers provide the variety and capacity needed for most any type or amount of waste.

Other special services that Waste Management provides for local business and industry are the safe reliable handling of nonhazardous industrial wastes. The availability of these services is critical in attracting and keeping vital industries that form the core economic base of the New Orleans metro area. The ability to provide the latest technology in waste management services was shown in recent economic studies to be a key factor in location decision models used by business and industry today. As the leader in solid waste management services, Waste Management of New Orleans plays an important role in the process that attracts and keeps the businesses and jobs that are so vital to the local economy.

In addition to the safe and efficient collection of solid waste materials from homes and commercial entities, the company also provides technical assistance to municipal sanitation departments and major industries; environmental engineering; generation of electricity from methane gas, a natural by-product of decomposition in landfills; the leas-

ing of portable sanitation facilities (Port-o-Lets); the creation and operation of water and wastewater treatment systems; and building demolition and disposal.

Making a Difference

Throughout the nation and around the world Waste Management's landfills are designed for future adaptation and use as public parks, golf courses, or other such applications that return the landfill to use as a community resource. In Louisiana a desired use is the return of the land to its wetland-habitat function, such as the landfill adjacent to the beautiful Bayou Sauvage National Wildlife Refuge in New Orleans. This facility was recently closed and capped, and is now used to access the refuge as an observation point for the annual bird count and as a part of the refuge land and water tours for visitors.

Waste Management of New Orleans also contributes to the quality of life in the city and region through monetary and in-kind service donations to civic and charitable organizations and causes. Among the many in-kind services of which Waste Management of New Orleans is most proud is the cleanup of the

city following each parade during the Mardi Gras season—a service that the company has provided pro bono to the city for more than 20 years.

For its many efforts and contributions, Waste Management of New Orleans has been recognized by many groups, among them the New Orleans Mayor's Office, City Council, and Parks and Parkways Commission; the cities of Kenner and Harahan; the parishes of St. Bernard and St. Charles; Christmas in October Restoration Project; Youth Action Corps; Lake Pontchartrain Basin Foundation; Louisiana Nature and Science Center; Audubon Institute; Volunteers of America; Multiple Sclerosis Foundation; and Preservation Resource Center.

Locally, nationally, and internationally, Waste Management's goal is to be caring and creative in its role as corporate citizen and to be the best, the safest, the cleanest, and the most efficient manager of our environment. Waste Management of New Orleans is proud of its quarter of a century of public-private partnership with the residents, businesses, and governmental entities in metro New Orleans and looks forward to another successful 25 years.

WASTE MANAGEMENT OF NEW ORLEANS' COMMERCIAL DIVISION SERVICES MANY OF THE PROMINENT BUSINESSES AND INDUSTRIES IN THE METRO AREA WITH FRONT-LOADING AND ROLL-OFF COLLECTION SERVICES.

TRUE SUCCESS IN THE WORLD OF ADVERTISING AND MARKETING IS A MATTER of unspoken recognition and acceptance by the business community. Since the earliest days of the firm's dramatic rise to success, Montgomery, Stire & Partners has been an integral part of the advertising community and business world in New Orleans and the southeastern United States. ✤ The firm's partners have invested great effort in supporting civic activities that contribute to an aesthetically and culturally healthy atmosphere in New Orleans, which, in turn, makes the city prosperous and is conducive to business success. George R. Montgomery—who has served as chairman of the Louisiana State Museum twice and as chairman of the Louisiana Museum Foundation and the Audubon Institute (whose complex of assets and activities have emerged as the city's premier tourist attraction), and who presently serves

on the board of the Arts Council of New Orleans and the Ochsner Medical Foundation—has made the well-being of New Orleans and Louisiana as much his business as the day-to-day operation of his agency. Frank E. Stire—also widely known for his civic activities, including his work with the Multiple Sclerosis Foundation and his leadership role with the Freeport-McDermott Golf Classic—is always able to find time in his schedule to participate in worthwhile community causes.

For more than two decades, Montgomery, Stire & Partners has built a solid reputation and performance record on the strength of creative and dedicated partners and staff members who represent years of experience and expertise in tourism/hospitality, entertainment, retail, and corporate image advertising and marketing. The agency provides a total mix of services required in today's concept of integrated market communications, which includes general marketing, database and incentive marketing, computer graphics, direct-response television, and public relations.

Partners

Montgomery, Stire & Partners believes in forming partnerships with clients—a true blending of roles and sharing of goals that invites client participation in the strategic and creative process. In return, the agency pledges marketing strategies that are fresh, clear, provocative, and persuasive. These strategies are designed to create or reinforce a unique personality for the client's product or service by using ideas that are simple, fast, and specific.

The agency is guided by the philosophy that the most precious commodity it has to sell is a fundamental understanding of a client/partner's target market and what motivates that market. "The tremendous explosion in cable, computers, and specialty magazines has brought changes in the nature of advertising," says Stire. "The customer, not the provider, now controls what he or she wants, and it is the customer, not the advertising agency, that dictates the message."

Total Marketing Concept

As an example of their integrated marketing approach, the agency tied its innovative direct-response television campaign for the City of New Orleans with media promotions and time-sharing agreements that stretched the client's ad budget and maximized the punch of every moment's exposure.

Along with the paid advertisements, the agency's public relations campaign for New Orleans Tourism created television and print publicity valued at $2.8 million in equivalent advertising rates. This unique approach ranks New Orleans as a leading example of marketing a city destination and is now widely imitated throughout the United States.

Perhaps most important, Montgomery, Stire & Partners recognizes the value of a client's money and time. The agency carefully analyzes costs and projected timetables in advance, sticks to budgets and schedules, and invites the client to ask "What am I getting for my advertising dollar?" throughout the process. "A true partner," both Stire and Montgomery agree, "could do no less."

GEORGE MONTGOMERY (LEFT) AND FRANK STIRE, FOUNDING PARTNERS OF MONTGOMERY, STIRE & PARTNERS, PROVIDE EXCELLENCE IN ADVERTISING, PUBLIC RELATIONS, AND MARKETING TO THE NEW ORLEANS AREA.

Royal Sonesta Hotel and Chateau Sonesta Hotel

ITH ONLY A SINGLE CITY BLOCK BETWEEN THEM, THE VENERABLE ROYAL Sonesta Hotel on Bourbon Street and the dazzling new Chateau Sonesta Hotel—with its Iberville, Dauphine, and Canal Street entrances—make New Orleans the only American city served by two Sonesta Hotel and Resort properties. Both have contributed immeasurably to preserving the ambience and architectural integrity of the Vieux Carré. The Royal

Sonesta rallied the state's leading restoration architects to recapture almost a full square block of the French Quarter. And the Chateau Sonesta saved the D.H. Holmes building—a landmark of Canal Street and a leading department store since 1849—from vacancy and an uncertain future.

President and General Manager Hans Wandfluh of the Royal Sonesta and General Manager Philippe Dubos of the Chateau Sonesta agree that the proximity of the properties creates an enhanced atmosphere and synergism rather than competition. The Swiss-born Wandfluh has spent 17 years of his

32-year hotel career in New Orleans and has raised his family here. The French-born Dubos considers his Chateau Sonesta assignment an "away-from-home homecoming," since this is his second New Orleans sojourn. He served the Royal Sonesta as director of food and beverage from 1980 to 1987.

Block Party
The Royal Sonesta is much more than a four-diamond hotel and convention property. The 500-room hotel and its resurrected block of the Vieux Carré have become home to such key elements of the Bourbon Street cityscape as the Desire Oyster Bar and Begue's Restaurant, which traces its tradition to Madame Elizabeth Begue's mid-19th-century restaurant near the French Market.

The Can-Can Cafe features the Silver Leaf Jazz Band, and the Mystick Den—with its year-round Mardi Gras spirit—offers still more jazz and overlooks the tropical courtyard. Many guest rooms overlook the courtyard and the endless festivities of Bourbon Street.

Holmes Sweet Holmes
The tiny shop that Daniel Holmes

opened at 22 Chartres in 1841 and moved to Canal Street in 1849 eventually grew to fill the four-story Italianate landmark that became the Chateau Sonesta in 1995. A grand experiment in the cooperation of federal, city, commercial, and civic resources for the promotion of downtown redevelopment, the Chateau Sonesta is a 250-room jewel that has won the hearts of not only its visitors but local preservationists as well.

The local tradition of meeting "under the clock at Holmes" was immortalized in the opening chapter of John Kennedy Toole's Pulitzer Prize-winning novel *A Confederacy of Dunces*, in which Ignatius Reilly waits there for his mother. The Chateau Sonesta and the city's Downtown Development District commissioned sculptor Bill Ludwig's statue of Ignatius for permanent placement "under the clock" at the Canal Street entrance.

The Sonestas of New Orleans provide visitors with an unparalleled experience through romantic courtyards, rooms with spectacular views of the French Quarter, and exquisite dining. All this is part of the distinctiveness of the first "new" French Quarter hotel to open in the past decade.

CLOCKWISE FROM TOP:
THE ROYAL SONESTA'S SPARKLING PINK-MARBLED LOBBY PROVIDES GUESTS WITH A MEMORABLE FIRST IMPRESSION.

THE CHATEAU SONESTA HOTEL WAS FORMERLY THE D.H. HOLMES DEPARTMENT STORE OF NEW ORLEANS, WHICH SERVICED THE CITY'S RESIDENTS FOR MORE THAN 140 YEARS.

THE CLOCK BAR OF THE CHATEAU SONESTA HOTEL IS NAMED AFTER THE FAMOUS D.H. HOLMES DEPARTMENT STORE CLOCK, FEATURED IN THE PULITZER PRIZE-WINNING NOVEL *A Confederacy of Dunces*. GENERATIONS OF NEW ORLEANIANS MET UNDER THE TIMEPIECE LOCATED ON CANAL STREET.

SONESTA HOTELS NEW ORLEANS EACH OFFER LUSH TROPICAL COURTYARDS WITH HEATED POOLS. PICTURED HERE ARE THE COURTYARDS OF THE ROYAL SONESTA HOTEL.

New Orleans Marriott

WHEN J. WILLARD MARRIOTT SR. TOURED NEW ORLEANS IN THE LATE 1960s, he was enchanted by the quaint city that seemed to have little trouble attracting visitors. Wanting to capitalize on the city's qualities, he built a towering convention hotel, complete with the largest ballroom in the state. ✦ The New Orleans Marriott opened its river tower in 1972, boasting 41 floors and 800 guest rooms, 18,000 square feet of exhibit space,

For the businessperson and conventioneer, the Marriott offers everything necessary for success, including flexible meeting and exhibit spaces, and stress-saving services such as Marriott Visual Presentations (right).

The view of the Mississippi River is dramatic through the windows of the Riverview Restaurant's southeast side, while the northeast windows offer an equally dramatic bird's-eye view of the French Quarter (below).

and more than 50,000 square feet of meeting and banquet space. With the 1976 addition of the quarter tower—which increased the hotel's size by 490 more guest rooms—plus the addition of the 27,089-square foot ballroom (the largest hotel ballroom in the city), the New Orleans Marriott became the largest Marriott hotel in the world, a distinction it held for years. Today, the hotel is the sixth largest, and will celebrate 25 years of being in business in 1997.

An Integral Part of the City

The Marriott's towers still stand proudly at their unique and enviable location, which overlooks the

nation's greatest river and faces the nation's broadest boulevard. In fact, the hotel is positioned so perfectly that it is, as its slogan proclaims, "Where the French Quarter Begins and the Good Times Never End." The Marriott is an indivisible part of the city and an integral part of the Canal Street cityscape. Like the street itself, the Marriott helps define the French Quarter, anchoring its upriver corner.

The Marriott is perfectly situated to provide easy access to all parts of the city. The heart of the French Quarter is within a short walking distance from the hotel via Decatur, Chartres, Royal, or Bourbon streets, and the riverfront is only

two blocks away. Tourists can walk two blocks on Canal Street to catch a St. Charles Avenue streetcar bound for the Central Business District or Garden District. They can also access the nearer reaches of the Central Business District by simply crossing Canal Street.

On the riverfront, in close proximity to the hotel, are the Canal Place shopping complex, the festive atmosphere of Riverwalk shopping, Audubon Zoo's new Aquarium of the Americas, and the IMAX Theater. From the riverfront, visitors can stroll the Woldenberg Riverfront Park route or catch a streetcar into the French Quarter; take a steamboat tour of the Port of New Orleans; or

THE CANAL STREET BAR IS A GREAT PLACE FOR INFORMAL SOCIALIZING AND PEOPLE-WATCHING.

even hop the free ferry to visit Mardi Gras World on the west bank of the Mississippi. From the Aquarium's dock, certain steamboats also regularly run upriver to the Audubon Zoo.

The great accessibility and convenience of the hotel's location produces unexpected visitor statistics at the Marriott. Despite its importance as a convention hotel, one-third of the Marriott's guests are tourists who have no convention or business-related agenda. Of course, no one comes to a convention in New Orleans just to talk business.

Amenities for the Entire Family

With the opening of the Aquarium, the IMAX Theater, the Rivertown Museum Complex in Kenner, the Louisiana Children's Museum in the Warehouse District, and the Louisiana Nature Center in New Orleans East, as well as the Carousel and Storyland renewal at City Park and the miraculous changes at the zoo, New Orleans has experienced a citywide shift in emphasis to family-oriented attractions. Many con-

ventioneers even bring their families to the city now, and the Marriott is ready to accommodate them.

The Marriott also caters to local residents who may wish to become tourists for a weekend by offering a room-and-breakfast package for those who want to explore the Quarter when it's alive with major events, such as the French Quarter Festival. Even at quieter times—when visitors wish to simply walk, dine, and listen to live music—the Marriott is the perfect place to start.

The hotel's Riverview Restaurant, 41 floors above the bend that gave the Crescent City its nickname, is a great reason to visit the Marriott. The view of the Mississippi River is dramatic through the windows of the restaurant's southeast side, while the northeast windows offer an equally dramatic bird's-eye view of the French Quarter. The restaurant offers a jazz brunch on Sundays, but great views of the sweeping cityscapes can be enjoyed at any time of the day.

For a bit of informality and people-watching, the hotel's gigantic lobby offers the Cafe du Marche,

featuring New Orleans specialties and American favorites; the Lobby Bar, with its evening jazz bands; and the Canal Street Bar, with access from both street and lobby.

The Gazebo Bar at poolside on the fifth-floor plaza, which is located between the hotel's two towers, offers cool southern and tropical drinks that are perfect for sunning and relaxing. Just down the corridor is the Marriott Health Club with its weight room, aerobics room, and saunas.

For the businessperson and conventioneer, the Marriott offers everything necessary for success, including flexible meeting and exhibit spaces, and stress-saving services such as Marriott Visual Presentations. In addition, the Marriott Business Center offers desktop publishing, printing, binding, and telecommunications services. For the casual visitor, the Marriott offers every convenience and luxury one would expect or desire for a carefree and comfortable vacation or a brief holiday escape—all provided with the best service that can be found as well as a little lagniappe in New Orleans.

Facing the French Quarter from Canal Street—anchoring the downriver corner of the central business district and overlooking the sweeping bend of the Mississippi River that gives the Crescent City its nickname—stand 17 floors of hospitality and comfort called the DoubleTree Hotel. ❧ The hotel is surrounded by jazz music, art galleries, carriage rides, antique shops, steamboat docks, and famous restaurants of "old" New

LARGE ENOUGH TO GUARANTEE EVERY SERVICE AND AMENITY A VISITOR MIGHT EXPECT FROM A FULL CONVENTION HOTEL, THE DOUBLETREE IS STILL SMALL ENOUGH TO BE COZY, AS THE DEN-LIKE INTIMACY OF ITS LOBBY DEMONSTRATES (RIGHT).

THE TRADEMARK OF THE 110-HOTEL DOUBLETREE FAMILY HAS BECOME THE HOME-BAKED CHOCOLATE CHIP COOKIES THAT VISITORS RECEIVE WHEN THEY CHECK IN. ACCORDING TO VETERAN DOUBLETREE TRAVELERS, THE COOKIES AT THE DOUBLETREE IN NEW ORLEANS ARE THE BEST OF ALL (BELOW).

Orleans just a few steps into the French Quarter. In addition, such contemporary attractions as the Aquarium of the Americas and the shopping of Canal Place and Riverwalk can all be found within a one-block stroll. Indeed, the DoubleTree's location is perfect for fun seekers and business travelers alike.

Large enough to guarantee every service and amenity a visitor might expect, the DoubleTree is still small enough to be cozy—from the denlike intimacy of its lobby to the romantic moonlit ambience of the

elegant top-floor International Ballroom, with its dramatic and panoramic view of the city and river.

In the Chips

If the 110 hotels of the DoubleTree family can be said to have a trademark, it would have to be the home-baked chocolate chip cookies that visitors receive when they check in. According to veteran DoubleTree travelers, the cookies at the Double-Tree in New Orleans are the best of all.

"It's a mystery even to us," admits General Manager Robert "Tico" Bevier, 1994-1995 president of the Louisiana Hotel-Motel Association, "but it's true. Same ingredients, same baking procedures, but they're just better here. People have always said New Orleans French bread can't be duplicated anywhere else—supposedly because of geographical latitude or sea-level altitude or some such factor—and I guess the same thing's true of our New Orleans chocolate chips."

Headquartered in Phoenix, with regional headquarters in Boston, the DoubleTree Hotel Corporation came to life in 1969 and merged with Guest Quarters Suite Hotels

in 1993 to form the fifth-largest hotel management company in the country. The DoubleTree Hotel in New Orleans, which took over management in 1973, is the corporation's number one property in terms of gross operating profit. And, with more than $15 million in annual sales, its corporate presence is a significant factor in the economic well-being of the community.

The DoubleTree's formula for success incorporates an unusual mix of qualities. While it has high service standards for creating smooth and pleasant business meeting experiences, the hotel maintains an equal measure of special attention and care that give it an unmistakable family orientation. The latter can be seen in its senior citizens' discounts and kids-stay-free policy.

Sweet Dreams

Guests discover the true meaning of the DoubleTree's "Sweet Dreams" motto when they wake up to a New Orleans morning in the comfort of their rooms. They may then choose from a host of luxuries provided by the hotel, which may begin with the five-minutes-or-free breakfast in the Chicory Rotisserie and Grille. They

can work out in the DoubleTree Fitness Center with its Stairmaster, treadmill, Life Cycle, and Universal equipment, or take a sun-and-swimming break at the fourth-floor pool deck. During the evening, they can enjoy a dinner of Cajun-inspired fowl, seafood, or roast in the Chicory Rotisserie and Grille, followed by cocktails in the hotel's Chicory Lounge.

The DoubleTree offers one of the most luxurious penthouse suites in the city, featuring such amenities as a baby grand piano, fireplace, sauna, Jacuzzi, French antiques, Italian crystal, and original artwork. In addition, the hotel offers one- and two-bedroom suites of various configurations.

CATERING TO THE CUSTOMER

The 20,000 square feet of meeting space at the DoubleTree allows flexibility in agenda planning, with spaces that range from the 700-seat International Ballroom to the smaller Crescent Ballroom to the secluded and exclusive meeting rooms for important roundtable discussions. In addition, the hotel has a complete business center, which provides full-service office support to business guests.

The hotel is capable of accommodating gatherings of almost any size, from the most intimate dinner to the most lavish event. In May 1996 the DoubleTree was the site of an extravaganza for the corporate

sponsors of the 1997 Superbowl XXXI. Attended by approximately 700, this event required the temporary transformation of the entire front of the hotel into a football stadium, complete with Astroturf featuring the Superbowl XXXI logo, goalposts, and the Vince Lombardi trophy carved in ice.

Whether a gathering is socially or business oriented, the DoubleTree offers a complete package of catering services. The hotel offers a full range of video equipment and technicians, special decorations, computer displays, sound equipment, security officers, and truly memorable meals and hors d'oeuvres.

A TRUE PARTNER TO THE COMMUNITY

The DoubleTree is active in supporting the New Orleans community. The hotel donates spaces, in conjunction with Ronald McDonald House, to the families of children who must visit New Orleans for serious hospital care. In addition, the hotel is an annual participant in the NO/AIDS Walk, for which it raised $3,000 in 1996. For the 1996 United Way campaign, the DoubleTree made the highest contribution per employee among New Orleans hotels. And, as part of the hotel's 10th anniversary celebration, the DoubleTree has adopted Each One Save One, a local children's mentoring agency.

New Orleans is a city with a nearly 300-year-old reputation for coddling its company, and the DoubleTree has done its best to keep that reputation intact.

FROM THE DOUBLETREE'S ENTRANCE ON CANAL STREET, GUESTS CAN EASILY WALK TO EVERYTHING NEW ORLEANS HAS TO OFFER (TOP).

THE HOTEL'S FOURTH-FLOOR POOL DECK CAN BE VERY REFRESHING TO VISITORS AFTER A FULL DAY OF MEETINGS AND ACTIVITIES (BOTTOM).

SIGMA COATINGS

HE HISTORY OF SIGMA COATINGS AND ITS PLANT ON THE HARVEY CANAL spans a quarter millennium and the world. Its origins date back to 1722, when Pieter Schoen of the Netherlands built a great windmill near Amsterdam that was specially geared for grinding pigments. Today, after nearly three centuries of leadership and innovation in the paints and protective coatings industry, Sigma employs 4,000 people worldwide; turns

a $1 billion annual revenue ($35 million in the United States); and has become a significant segment of Petrofina, the multinational Belgian conglomerate that founded Sigma in 1969.

LOCAL COLOR

Sigma's four business sectors consist of decorative paints, coil coatings, general industry coatings, and marine and protective coatings. The marine and protective coatings branch has expanded to include locations around the world, with New Orleans as its U.S. business and production center. A manufacturer of alkyds, epoxies, coal tar epoxies, polyurethanes, and waterborne acrylics, Sigma was drawn to New Orleans because of the area's concentration of marine, petrochemical, and offshore indus-tries, all of which are prime users of such products.

In 1976 the company purchased Standard Paint and Varnishes from Avondale Shipyard, which had been manufacturing marine paints for Sigma under license. In 1992 it made the move to its sprawling new facility in the shadow of the Westbank Expressway's Harvey Canal bridge, demonstrating its commitment to growth in the U.S. marketplace.

Since its arrival, Sigma's coat-ings have beautified and protected such high-visibility surfaces as the high-rise steel elements of the Crescent City Connection; Baton

Rouge's Interstate-10 bridge; petro-leum tanks in Geismar; sugar mills in St. Mary Parish; thousands of rail-cars traveling the tracks of America; and scores of industrial plants and oil rigs throughout Louisiana, the Gulf Coast, and the Gulf of Mexico.

Thanks to Sigma's research and development labs in Europe and its dedicated New Orleans scientists, who develop, fine-tune, and adapt products to meet specific regional requirements, Sigma is able to offer itself as a "corrosion-protection partner" to local industry, protecting valuable assets in steel and concrete for 15, 20, or even more years per application. The high-technology epoxy coatings meet all local and international environmental stan-dards while creating a barrier coat that withstands the elements better and longer than Schoen could ever have imagined. In addition, by focusing on cost-effective superior-performing products designed to meet the specific application and performance requirements of the rail-car industry, Sigma has gained a lead-ership position in this U.S. market.

The goal of Sigma, which now produces up to 10,000 gallons of its products per day, is to bring about a 50 percent increase in sales over the next five years, not only through its continued marketing and produc-tion successes, but also through expansion of the product line by the introduction of additional innovative

and environmentally safe products each year. Also, with its world leader-ship position in tanklinings, Sigma continues to introduce leading-edge technology/100 percent solids/ solvent-free linings products with broad cargo-carrying capability and with very user-friendly application characteristics.

PROTECTING THE FUTURE

The company slogan, "Protecting the Future," carries the obvious implication of maximizing the life of any structural surface or piece of equipment to which Sigma's prod-ucts are applied. More than that, it carries the promise of the compa-ny's continuing commitment to the development of innovative, environmentally safe, and superior performing products that provide longer-term asset protection in fewer coats, thus minimizing application costs and reducing the client's long-term maintenance budget.

EYE SURGERY CENTER OF LOUISIANA

THE DAY IS RAPIDLY APPROACHING WHEN THE ONLY PEOPLE WHO WILL WEAR glasses or contacts will be those who choose to do so. Dr. Stephen F. Brint, medical director of the Eye Surgery Center of Louisiana, believes that day may come as soon as the year 2000. "Most patients who walk through our doors are appropriate candidates for a surgical procedure to correct their refractive error," says Brint. "Technology is moving ahead so rapidly that

we should be able to correct most forms of refractive error by the end of the century."

Brint, a Louisiana native, graduated in 1972 from the Tulane School of Medicine, where he still serves as associate clinical professor of ophthalmology. He founded the Eye Surgery Center of Louisiana in 1977 and surrounded himself with skilled clinicians, surgeons, and experts in the diagnosis and treatment of vision disorders of every type. Through his continuous involvement with eye surgery techniques, Brint is at the forefront in development and testing of new techniques in the field.

LASER REVOLUTION

A godsend to many people at the time it was developed (nearly 20 years ago), radial keratotomy (RK) was subject to the same lack of precision as any surgical procedure. Improvements soon followed with new procedures such as astigmatic keratectomy (AK); automated lamellar keratoplasty (ALK); and, after several years of clinical trials by Brint at the Eye Surgery Center of Louisiana and investigators at 10 other U.S. sites, excimer laser photorefractive keratotomy (PRK). Two laser systems, Summit and Visx, have been approved by the Food and Drug Administration for use in the United States in treating mild to moderate nearsightedness using PRK. The Eye Surgery Center of Louisiana is the first and only facility in the Gulf South to house the only FDA-approved lasers, Summit and Visx.

The most recent procedure to be developed utilizing the precision and predictability of the excimer is called laser assisted in situ keratomileusis (LASIK). Brint was the

first surgeon in the United States to perform this procedure, which involves no treatment on the surface of the cornea. With LASIK, the outer few microns of the cornea are partially resected, creating a hinged flap that is first lifted, allowing the laser to perform its reshaping inside, and then replaced, with no disruption to the surface tissue. There is no discomfort during healing and none of the brief haziness or other visual abnormality occasionally associated with the healing of PRK, which treats the surface.

"LASIK is effective on higher amounts of myopia than any of the refractive procedures," says Brint. "Many cases considered inappropriate for RK and PRK can now

be reevaluated. Of course, FDA approval—which has been our goal—means that hundreds of patients can now have the LASIK procedure and have clearer vision."

In looking toward the future, Brint foresees a time when artificial lenses inserted within the eye will correct nearsightedness and, eventually, farsightedness for many. He has already had hands-on experience with the procedure in Mexico and plans to participate when it is tested during the next century in the United States. Through the skills and knowledge gained from the tireless efforts of Brint and his staff, the Eye Surgery Center of Louisiana will soon be able to provide corrected vision that can last a lifetime.

DR. STEPHEN F. BRINT, FOUNDER AND MEDICAL DIRECTOR OF THE EYE SURGERY CENTER OF LOUISIANA, IS AT THE FOREFRONT OF DEVELOPING AND TESTING NEW TECHNIQUES IN CORRECTIVE EYE SURGERY.

GREAT BUILDINGS ARE OFTEN A REFLECTION OF THE TIME AND PLACE IN which they were built. This is especially true in the case of the New Orleans Hilton Riverside. Built in three phases and over three decades, the Hilton has been a symbol for three significant eras in the recent history of New Orleans. ✤ The city's two most dramatic bursts of urban development in the late 20th century were the Poydras Street boom of the 1970s and the riverfront rediscovery of the 1980s. Poised at the very spot where Poydras meets the riverfront, the Hilton became an integral part of both movements by opening its Tower section in 1977 and its Riverside Building in 1983. And during the third important era, when the 1990s brought riverboat gaming to the area, the Hilton's steamboat, the Flamingo Casino New Orleans, was the first afloat.

GUESTS AT THE NEW ORLEANS HILTON RIVERSIDE CAN ENJOY PO'BOYS, JAMBALAYA, AND MUFFU-LETTAS AT KABBY'S SPORTS EDITION AND GRILLE WHILE CATCHING THE GAME ON SOME OF THE 52 SATELLITE-FED TELEVISIONS (RIGHT).

BUILT IN THREE PHASES AND OVER THREE DECADES, THE HILTON HAS BEEN A SYMBOL FOR THREE SIGNIFICANT ERAS IN THE RECENT HISTORY OF NEW ORLEANS (BELOW).

The Tower

In addition to its original 1,150 guest rooms and suites, the Tower features 144 concierge-class rooms and suites on its top four floors, which offer picturesque views and special amenities such as access to the Towers Lounge with its delicious breakfasts, hors d'oeuvres, and cocktails.

Pete Fountain's Club features the world-famous jazz clarinetist, while Cafe Bromeliad in the Tower's atrium offers buffets and Sunday jazz brunches. Le Croissant offers à la carte dining during the morning and early afternoon hours.

Down by the Riverside

The Riverside Building runs up and down the river to more than a dozen open-air plazas that provide views of streetcars on one side of the building and steamboats and ferryboats on the other. The building's second-floor entrance area also provides access to the Flamingo Casino and stairway access to the Riverwalk.

Popular Kabby's on the River, located on the building's second floor, serves Cajun and Creole spe-cialties and boasts the city's most intimate view of the Mississippi River. Those who would prefer to view some sports action can enjoy po'boys, jambalaya, and muffulettas at Kabby's Sports Edition and Grille, while catching the game on some of the 52 satellite-fed televisions.

Work and Play

Hilton guests have access to the hotel's RiverCenter Racquet and Health Club, which is one of the five largest health spas in the nation, featuring eight indoor tennis courts, four racquetball courts, three squash courts, a basketball court, golf studio, exercise complex, tanning salon, saunas, massage therapy, and whirlpools.

For conventioneers, the Hilton offers covered access via the River-walk to the New Orleans Conven-tion Center. In addition, the hotel has 127,000 square feet of function space, including 38 meeting rooms, the 22,000-square-foot Exhibition Center, 26,894-square-foot Grand Ballroom, and 24,179-square-foot Grand Salon. The Business Center in the Riverside Building provides dic-tation, computer, desktop publishing, and communications services.

The Hilton is a traditional lodging place for Sugar Bowl, Superbowl, and Final Four teams; for Crescent City Classic runners; and for Mardi Gras krewe members whose balls are held in or near the hotel. And it is the choice of nearly 1 million visitors a year who just want great facilities in a great loca-tion in a great vacation and conven-tion town.

HARRY KELLEHER & CO., INC.
INSURANCE AND EMPLOYEE BENEFITS

I T CAN BE SAID THAT HARRY KELLEHER & CO. GOT ITS START IN 1963, WHEN President and Founder Harry B. Kelleher Jr. graduated from Tulane University and was awarded a College of Insurance-New York Certificate. For the next 13 years, while rising to the position of executive vice president of a local insurance agency, Kelleher honed his skills and realized his personal goal of creating an organization of his own that would excel

at risk analysis and insurance protection plans for individuals and corporations. Since opening the doors at Harry Kelleher & Co., Inc. in 1984, Kelleher has built his own company by applying the invaluable knowledge he gained through years of experience.

STRONG LEADERSHIP
A member of the Professional Insurance Agents of America, the Louisiana Association of Life Underwriters, and Independent Agents of Greater New Orleans and Louisiana, Kelleher is also active in civic and community affairs. He is a member of the Chamber-New Orleans and the River Region and the Louisiana Association of Business and Industry; past chairman of the Tulane Medical Center Board of Governors; past development chairman of the Audubon Park Commission; former alumni trustee of the Lawrenceville School; and secretary of the Libby Dufour Fund.

Having joined the company in 1985, Senior Vice President W. Patrick Kelleher is certified as a chartered property casualty underwriter (CPCU) and an associate in risk management (ARM). Drawing on years of underwriting experience in a large risk department and in the mass marketing of commercial accounts, he received the coveted Associate in Marine Insurance Management (AMIM) designation.

Rounding out the principals of the agency is Vice President of Commercial Lines and Agency Finance Gerard F. Ryder, who is a graduate of Loyola University and the Travelers Insurance Company's Commercial Lines School for Agents, and Executive Vice President Harry B. Kelleher III, who graduated from

Hampden-Sidney College and the United States Fidelity and Guaranty underwriting training program. In all, the agency is run by 12 sales staff members and 10 service representatives, all of whom are licensed in Louisiana and specialize in specific areas of insurance coverage.

THREE PS
The formula for success at Harry Kelleher & Co., Inc., which has tripled its volume to $12 million in the past five years, is called the "Three Ps Philosophy." This includes personalized service for the client, utilizing years of experience pinpointing aspects of risk that are unique to contractors, marine operations, hotels, manufacturers, and professionals; professional development by encouraging, recognizing, and rewarding an agent's quest for broader expertise in the world of insurance protection; and "processing made easy," which involves develop-

ment of computerized systems for the highly complex and volatile risk-evaluation requirements of today's changing business world.

"When it comes to corporate coverage, we develop real friendships with our clients and a genuine interest in the success of their companies," says Harry B. Kelleher Jr. "We assume a huge responsibility when we analyze a person's individual needs or evaluate a company's exposure. When an unfortunate occurrence arises, proper protection may save a company by providing the resources necessary to continue its operations uninterrupted."

To that end, Kelleher agents work closely with underwriters to create specialty coverage for specific needs, such as Kelleher's competitive and very comprehensive coverage developed for large-scale hotel operations. In short, the three Ps could be summed up with only one—protecting the client.

◀ MICHAEL P. SMITH

THE PRINCIPALS AT HARRY KELLEHER & CO., INC. ARE (FROM LEFT) W. PATRICK KELLEHER, CPCU, ARM; HARRY B. KELLEHER III; HARRY B. KELLEHER JR., CPIA; AND GERARD F. RYDER.

Williams & Associates Architects

THE WORLD OF ARCHITECT JOHN WILLIAMS IS ALL-ENCOMPASSING: It is as tiny as the Cajun cottage exhibit in the Louisiana Children's Museum and as vast as the Port of New Orleans, whose master plan is among his special ongoing interests, and the Villa Meilleur, an 1828 Treme cottage that he transformed into the city's new Museum of African-American Art. Williams' works are as private as restorations to homes on St. Charles Avenue and

the French Quarter and as public as the Russell Senate Office Building in Washington, D.C.; as youthful and radiant as the New Orleans Children's Museum and as seasoned and luminous as the century-old Tiffany triptychs at Newcomb College's

WILLIAMS & ASSOCIATES HAS BECOME AN INTERNATIONALLY RENOWNED ORGANIZATION AND HAS DEVELOPED SUCH PROJECTS AS EMERIL'S RESTAURANT AT 800 TCHOUPITOULAS STREET (ABOVE) AND THE TUTTON RESIDENCE AT 521 GOVERNOR NICHOLLS STREET (RIGHT).

Woldenberg Center at Tulane University. In essence, Williams' world is the world itself, and he and his firm, Williams & Associates Architects, have contributed greatly to its structures, particularly in New Orleans.

A Hand in All Areas

For many local residents, it might be easier to recognize the major New Orleans projects that Williams & Associates Architects has designed or collaborated on than to name ones that it has not. Starting in 1983 with nine architects and three interior designers, Williams & Associates has become an internationally renowned organization and has developed such commercial and retail projects as Emeril's Restaurant, Bella Luna Restaurant, the prototype for Catfish Charlie Restaurants, Gentlemen's Quarter, Morton's Auction Ex-

change, and the upcoming Maison Blanche Building conversion into a luxury hotel.

Williams' residential work spans from the historic Lower Pontalba Building apartments to the East Capitol Carbarn condominiums in Washington, D.C. The firm's public buildings and spaces include Bienville Place/Conti Park, New Orleans Recreational Department's new Conrad Park, Boys Town of New Orleans, Newcomb College's Woldenberg Art Center, Trinity Episcopal Church and school, seven schools, two libraries, Whitney and First NBC bank projects, the Covington Office Park, and dozens of individual office spaces for professionals and businesses. Medical-related work includes projects for the American Cancer Society, New Orleans Speech and Hearing Clinic,

246   NEW ORLEANS:

Planned Parenthood of Louisiana, West Jefferson General Hospital, and various dental and medical clinics.

John Williams' personal involvement includes service on numerous master-planning boards, including those of the New Orleans Medical Complex, the University of New Orleans' Research and Technology Park, the Port of New Orleans, and the Downtown Development District's Loyola and Canal Street planning groups. He has participated in developing growth management plans for the City of New Orleans under three mayors, and he has served on the mayor's public housing transition team and on several housing project task forces.

Membership and committee work with the Vieux Carré Commission—which works to protect the French Quarter—is a labor of love for Williams, for whom historic preservation and adaptive restoration are passions as well as professional pursuits. "It's really exciting," says Williams, "to dig into a project when the old building is really a good one and worthy of restoration. You get to know every square inch, finding evidence of what the builders, designers, and renovators have done to the structure before you. You might move a wall for the sake of some modern necessity, but you try to do it artfully, re-creating period details and the like to make your changes seem natural and proper."

PSYCHOLOGY TODAY

Before he decided to pursue architecture as a profession, Williams earned a degree in psychology, which, he believes, serves him well in his current endeavors. "I think it taught me how to understand people and how to ask the right questions, and that's really the secret to good design— being able to learn from a client what it is that he or she really wants, expects, and needs," says Williams. He is also known for his ability to accurately judge what projects will cost and how to juggle each client's budget, expectations, and needs in order to achieve the best possible result.

"Great architecture, contrary to popular opinion, is not related to an enormous price tag," Williams says. "It's the desire to perform perfectly, at the highest level of professional qualifications—whether it's a $20,000 project or $20 million, a single room or a great hospital, improvements at a housing project or a master plan for an entire city. It's the determination to make the best decisions possible so that, even if it's simply someone's garage, it will be the most perfect garage possible in terms of function and design within the context of its surrounding environment."

PARTNERS IN PROGRESS

Williams and his wife, Laura, are aware of the needs and potential of their community, and they involve themselves in effecting positive change in every aspect of their surroundings. Despite the obligations of career and family, they serve on the vestry of Trinity Church as well as on its Task Force for the Homeless and Low-Income Housing Task Force. They also participate in numerous meetings and activities with boards and advisory groups for school, neighborhood, and city improvement. They exhibit the vision and energy required to conceive worthwhile projects, inspire action committees, and then watch with satisfaction as the fruits of their labors become part of the fabric of life in the city.

"New Orleans gets to be so much a part of you," says Williams of his city. "It always will be, even though more and more of our work is becoming national and international."

THE FIRM'S COMMERCIAL AND RETAIL PROJECTS INCLUDE (CLOCKWISE FROM TOP) THE FIRST AMERICAN TITLE INSURANCE COMPANY HEADQUARTERS, BELLA LUNA RESTAURANT, AND 541 DECATUR STREET IN NEW ORLEANS.

STEWART & STEVENSON SERVICES, INC.

OR ALMOST A CENTURY STEWART & STEVENSON SERVICES, INC. HAS BEEN the supplier of numerous types of machinery that has become indispensable to many of America's key industries. Its products include tactical vehicles for the military and giant generators that power offshore oil rigs and provide backup power for hospitals. The company is the world's largest manufacturer of well-stimulation apparatuses, including fracturing equipment, blenders, chemical additive systems, and acidizing equipment, all of which improve flow from oil and gas reservoirs.

Stewart & Stevenson is also a major manufacturer of such drilling equipment as blowout preventers, riser-pipe connections, high-pressure valves, coiled tubing units, surface wellheads, and the like. Through the collective successes of its market segments, the company earned an impressive $1.23 billion in sales in 1995.

THREE SEGMENTS

Operating both nationally and internationally, Stewart & Stevenson's activities are divided into three primary company divisions, the first of which is responsible for custom design and engineering of engine systems for the generation of electrical and mechanical power. This includes gas- and diesel-driven generator sets for primary and standby electrical power, and special applications for the petroleum and airline markets.

The distribution segment of the company's activities involves the marketing of industrial equipment and related parts from the Electro-Motive Division of General Motors (EMD); MTU; and manufacturers such as Detroit Diesel, John Deere, Waukesha, Allison Transmission, and others. In New Orleans Stewart & Stevenson plays an important role in the local marine business, selling propulsion systems and power-generating systems for tugboats, supply vessels, patrol boats, yachts, and drilling rigs, all primarily using Detroit Diesel, EMD, and MTU engines. The company also provides in-house and on-site repair services for ships and other vessels. Its strategic location on the Harvey Canal provides an ideal point of access to those needing its services. The division also provides power generation and other equipment for oil, gas, and other industry customers, utilizing diesel engines and dual fuel and natural-gas-powered engines. In addition, complete financing packages can be arranged for clients on a per project basis.

The tactical vehicle segment manufactures the U.S. Army's Family of Medium Tactical Vehicles (FMTVs), which include 2.5- and five-ton trucks configured as troop carriers, wreckers, cargo trucks, vans, and dump trucks.

HOME WORK

Stewart & Stevenson established its foothold in New Orleans nearly a decade ago by purchasing the

THIS 135-FOOT ALUMINUM CREW BOAT, POWERED BY DETROIT DIESEL ENGINES AND GENERATORS, LEFT NEW ORLEANS AND RAN TO SAUDI ARABIA ON ITS OWN POWER.

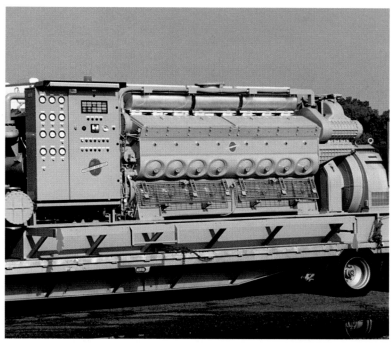

structures and prime location of George Engine Company, Inc. Situated on the Harvey Canal, the local plant now serves as headquarters of the company's Gulf Coast Division.

The New Orleans plant is led by Regional Director Ralston Cole, who received his engineering training at Tulane University and the U.S. Naval Academy, and his graduate training at Louisiana State University. Having risen from his position as sales engineer to vice president of sales at George Engine in the late 1960s and early 1970s, Cole brought a valuable working knowledge of the facility with him when Stewart & Stevenson set up shop and coaxed him back to head the local and regional operation in 1988.

The primary mission of Stewart & Stevenson's 220 employees in New Orleans is the manufacture, marketing, installation, and servicing of the giant power generation units for which the company is famous. In addition, the company offers generator rental service; a repair and overhaul shop for engines and transmissions for large transport trucks that arrive via the Westbank Expressway; a service center for vessels that access the facility via the Harvey Canal; and a huge parts department for support of all generator, truck,

marine, and oil field servicing operations.

Stewart & Stevenson's canal-side Field Service Facility houses the company's administrative and sales offices, as well as the giant garages and shops that are designed to service visiting vessels and 18-wheel trailer trucks. The facility also features shops for handling the remanufacture of power-pack parts, as well as for the service and repair of all large and small machinery produced by the company's petroleum equipment division. The Field Service Facility in New Orleans is one of three Stewart & Stevenson service centers in the world that are equipped to service such a staggering variety of machinery products.

Near the Field Service Facility stands the gigantic Fab Shop, which houses the company's modification and fabrication operations. In this facility approximately 600 monolithic generator sets are produced each year, some of which are large enough to power battleships. In fact, many of these generator sets are destined for military and commercial vessels. The diesel and turbine engines that power these generators are purchased from such manufacturers as the Electro-Motive Division of General Motors, Detroit Diesel, Waukesha, Superior,

Ruston, Spectrum, and Generac. These engines are installed as the core power source within Stewart & Stevenson's generation units, which are custom-designed and assembled to exacting specifications for installation in ships, buildings, drilling platforms, and wherever large-scale power generation is required.

In 1996 Stewart & Stevenson entered into an agreement to build and sell preengineered barge-mounted gas turbine generators for POWERBARGE™ units, which are designed and constructed at McDermott shipyard and which will offer the rapid delivery and start-up capabilities required for the power-generation needs of many international customers.

OUTLOOK

Stewart & Stevenson is facing the new millennium with great optimism, based on current trends in local and world markets. The resurgence of drilling activities in Louisiana and the Gulf of Mexico certainly bodes well for the company's myriad oil field support sales and servicing activities. In addition, the transition to a more competitive worldwide electric utility market is expected to create great opportunities to sell gas turbines and reciprocating engines, both domestically and internationally.

EMD MODEL 16-645E1 16-CYLINDER 1500KW DIESEL GENSET (TOP)

THE HARVEY CANAL OFFERS THE NEW ORLEANS BRANCH A UNIQUE OPPORTUNITY TO PROVIDE ITS CUSTOMERS WITH TRUE DOCKSIDE SERVICE. THE BRANCH HAS 1,300 FEET OF DOCK SPACE, WHICH ALLOWS YACHTS, CREW BOATS, AND SUPPLY BOATS TO TIE UP FOR SUPERIOR SERVICE (BELOW).

L OCATED IN THE HEART OF NEW ORLEANS IS A SPRAWLING CLUSTER OF medical facilities where a new spirit of cooperation between well-established independent institutions is making visible contributions to the cityscape and the quality of life in New Orleans. Founded in 1991, the New Orleans Medical Complex (NORMC), an outgrowth of a medical task force formed in 1989 by the Downtown Development District, is a nonprofit

entity whose purpose is to coordinate efforts by member institutions to promote collective excellence in health care delivery, education, research, and economic development.

The complex is comprised of the Medical Center of Louisiana, Louisiana State University (LSU) Medical Center, Tulane University Medical Center, Veterans Affairs Medical Center, Xavier University College of Pharmacy, Louisiana Office of Public Health, Downtown Development District, and a host of other health-related offices, organizations, agencies, and clinics.

Mission Possible

The goals of the New Orleans Medical Complex are to provide safe and pleasant medical facilities for the citizens of New Orleans and its visitors, support biomedical research, and promote the complex as a premier medical center. In addition, the complex also provides a meeting ground for synergy and cooperation among its member facilities.

The long-range master plan of NORMC calls for a wide variety of steps designed to create a unified medical campus. The first step is to improve the Interstate-10/Claiborne Avenue corridor with the goal of creating an enhanced pedestrian and vehicular zone including high-visibility portals into the complex. In the future the complex's member institutions plan to share multistory parking garages and interconnecting second-floor walkways and street crossings. This project is already under way, thanks to a $1 million grant from the Louisiana Department of Transportation and Development and $300,000 in Phase II funds. New landscaping

and signage for Claiborne Avenue intersections are being developed, as have logo-bearing trash receptacles, Medical Complex banners, trailblazer signs that lead to buildings

and parking facilities, and improved pedestrian crosswalks.

Public art and miniparks will further enhance the spirit of the surrounding area. In addition, the

pride instilled by a series of television advertisements promoting the complex has motivated both public and private community participation in improvement projects.

Various committees of NORMC are currently studying areas of possible cost sharing among members through, for example, computer networking and centralized databases. One early achievement has been the creation of a police/security task force, which has reached agreements of cooperation, established a quarterly lighting inventory to identify and correct inadequate lighting, and agreed on a common radio frequency for monitoring by police and security personnel. As a result, crime in the district has been significantly reduced.

SELLING ITSELF

One continuing function of the complex will be its Clinical Investment Unit, which will market the expertise of research personnel and facilities. One traditional strategy, manning booths at medical conventions and conferences, can actually be done without ever leaving the city; New Orleans hosts more medical events each year than any other U.S. city, and every major medical society is a regular convention guest here.

The complex also supports the efforts of the University of New Orleans' Business Incubator Program, which can help turn lab discoveries into commercial successes by introducing innovations to manufacturers and distributors. One project that promises to have far-reaching results is the development of commercial properties between and around member facilities—a 40-block area bounded by Loyola Avenue, Iberville, Galvez, and Julia streets—into the Louisiana Biomedical Research and Development Park. The area has been established as a tax-free haven for medical and biomedically related commercial ventures that can benefit from the collaboration opportunities with the academic medical centers. With $150,000 from the city's

economic development fund, the complex has amassed a site database of all property within its boundaries. The database provides a detailed registry of 100 buildings that total 6 million square feet of building space.

The success of the research park should provide a boost to the entire economy, since the park is predicted to create more than 2,250 new positions in its early years. For every medical researcher, 35 other jobs will be created in support positions and related fields.

The New Orleans Medical Complex is well on its way to a promising future that will enhance the lives of New Orleans residents. Through the collective achievements of its member institutions, the complex will continue to provide outstanding health care services to the community while also contributing a magnet for growth and prosperity.

▲ THE CHAMBER/NEW ORLEANS AND THE RIVER REGION

▲ IRVING JOHNSON, XAVIER UNIVERSITY

NORMC IS ABLAZE WITH LIGHTS. AS THE HUB OF MEDICAL HEALTH CARE IN THE CITY OF NEW ORLEANS, THE COMPLEX PROVIDES FACILITIES THAT ALLOW THE ART OF HEALING TO BE PRACTICED AROUND THE CLOCK (ABOVE).

BASIC SCIENCE RESEARCH IS AT THE CORE OF EMERGING TECHNOLOGIES FOR THE CONTINUED IMPROVEMENT OF CARE PROVIDED AT THE BEDSIDE. PATIENTS IN NORMC BENEFIT FROM THE VAST RESEARCH CARRIED OUT AT THE DOWNTOWN MEDICAL COMPLEX (LEFT).

AT THE TURN OF THE CENTURY, JAZZ MUSICIANS MADE THEIR LIVING playing in the establishments of the famous Storyville district of North Rampart and Basin streets. But it was in the South Rampart-Perdido area that they lived their daily lives. The district and its role in the story of New Orleans jazz might be a distant memory now, were it not for a monument that rises 18 stories above the few remaining landmarks of that era: the

RESPECT FOR NEW ORLEANS' JAZZ HISTORY IS REFLECTED THROUGHOUT THE HOLIDAY INN DOWNTOWN-SUPERDOME. ROBERT DAFFORD OF LAFAYETTE WAS COMMISSIONED TO CREATE THE STUNNING TROMPE L'OEIL, A 150-FOOT EXTERIOR MURAL OF A CLARINET (BOTTOM LEFT), AND NUMEROUS LIFE-SIZE STREET SCENES THAT DEPICT ACTUAL BUILDINGS AND FACES ASSOCIATED WITH THE AREA'S HEYDAY (TOP LEFT AND BOTTOM RIGHT).

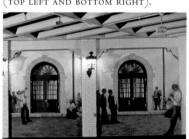

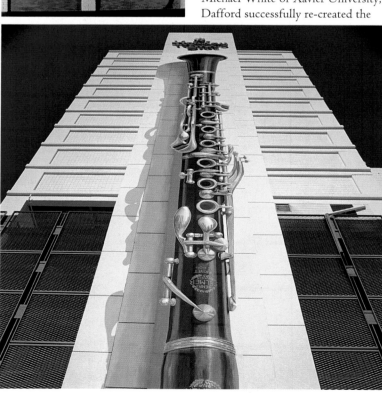

Holiday Inn Downtown-Superdome, which is located at 330 Loyola Avenue. The hotel pays homage to the city's jazz heritage through its fantastic Buddy Bolden Breezeway and the stunning trompe l'oeil—a 150-foot exterior mural of a clarinet—both of which offer a preview of the delights that await jazz and art lovers inside the hotel.

PRESERVING THE PAST

Robert Dafford of Lafayette—who has created murals on façades, seawalls, and other gigantic "canvases" worldwide—was commissioned by the Holiday Inn to create the 16-story clarinet and life-size street scenes. Utilizing research assistance from Don Marquis, curator of the New Orleans Jazz Club Collections of the Louisiana State Museum, and Dr. Michael White of Xavier University, Dafford successfully re-created the

spirit and excitement of the actual birthplace of jazz in New Orleans while maintaining strict superrealism in his depiction of a pre-1920 Selmer "Albert System" clarinet. His street scenes preserve actual buildings and faces associated with the area's heyday—including Louis Armstrong, Buddy Bolden, Joe "King" Oliver, Kid Ory, Sidney Bechet, and dozens more.

The Holiday Inn's respect for New Orleans' jazz history is reflected throughout the 300-room hotel—from the Preservation Hallway and the banquet rooms to oil paintings of jazzmen by Stig Marcussen and the eighth-floor Bayou Ballroom's reception area, which features Marcussen's series of oils depicting Louisiana swamp and marsh scenes. Within the lobby and Holiday Streetcar Restaurant, which serves lunch buffets, dinner specials, and live Maine lobster, Marcussen's paintings depict various eras and neighborhoods in the more than 160-year history of streetcars in New Orleans.

Cajun and zydeco are certainly part of New Orleans' musical heritage. Each of the hotel's elevator

landings captures the spirit of Cajun music and dancing as depicted through the series of paintings by local artist Daniel Breaux.

The Mardi Gras Lounge features local artist Shirley Masinter's vibrant oil paintings of Carnival, along with the costumes worn by owner Dian Winingder and her husband when they were Queen and King of the Krewe of Iris. Mardi Gras music and decor make the lounge a year-round haven for Carnival lovers and visitors.

A FEW SURPRISES

Since it is located within close proximity of many important downtown destinations—including the French Quarter, City Hall, the Louisiana Supreme Court, the Superdome, the Central Business District, and the New Orleans Medical Complex—the Holiday Inn has had little trouble maintaining a high and constant occupancy rate. Those who visit this Loyola Avenue hotel find "a cozy little property with a few surprises," in the words of Fortuné Jaubert, the hotel's general manager. He has led his property to an unprecedented two consecutive Holiday Inn Worldwide Quality Excellence Awards, the 1996 International Award for Marketing Innovation, and the 1995-1996 Holiday Inn Renovation Award.

The Holiday Inn Downtown-Superdome is committed to preserving the heritage that has helped make New Orleans a destination city. And through its high-quality service, festive atmosphere, and top-notch amenities, the Holiday Inn Downtown-Superdome will be remembered by guests for years to come as a place of convenience, comfort, "and all that jazz."

PHOTOGRAPHERS

PATRICK CONE is an award-winning photographer and writer living in Oakley, Utah, who has also served as a helicopter navigator and geophysicist. From unique aerial and land-based perspectives, Cone photographs avalanches, active volcanoes, forest fires, and other natural phenomena. The author and photographer of *Nature in Action: Grand Canyon!* and the photographer of *Nature in Action: Avalanche!*—two children's titles from CarolRhoda Books (Minneapolis)—Cone is currently writing the next two books in that series.

ROSEMARIE A. DOUMITT, a New Orleans resident since 1988, is a Jackson, Tennessee, native whose creative work ranges from fine art imagery to documentary to a combination of the two. While working on her graduate degree in photography, Doumitt completed thesis work on nudes in the landscape. Most recently she has worked as a freelance photographer for the New Orleans Ballet and the *Times-Picayune*, as well as a teacher of photography.

PHILIP GOULD, a cultural documentary photographer, has made Louisiana his home and favorite subject over the past two decades. Based in Cajun country near Grand Coteau, he has taken photographs throughout the state. His work has resulted in one of the largest individual photographic archives of contemporary Louisiana and has been published in numerous books, magazines, and exhibits over the years. Most recently Gould was awarded the 1996 Louisiana Governor's Arts Award for Professional Artist of the Year.

JACKSON HILL, a native of Mobile, Alabama, moved to New Orleans in 1980. A longtime member of the American Society of Media Photographers and the National Press Photographers Association, he specializes in magazine and advertising photography, digital imaging, and World Wide Web site construction. Hill's clients include *Forbes, Fortune, Business Week, Time,* and *Rolling Stone* magazines,

as well as Amnesty International. He maintains a large body of work on the Internet at www.southernlights.com.

DAVE G. HOUSER is an award-winning travel journalist who has visited more than 125 countries. Specializing in offbeat and adventure, cruise and luxury travel, personality, health, and history photography, he is a contributing editor to *Vacations* and *Cruises & Tours* magazines and a coauthor of the travel guidebook *Hidden Coast of California*. Houser was the 1985 runner-up for the Lowell Thomas Travel Journalist of the Year Award and was named the 1984 Society of American Travel Writers' Photographer of the Year.

JACK KENNER, a native of Memphis, Tennessee, is the owner of Jack Kenner Photography Studio and Take a Closer Look Photographic Gallery, located in Overton Square. In addition to earning a scholarship to study in Santa Barbara, where he received his bachelor of fine arts degree, Kenner has studied at the Brooks Institute of Photography and the University of Memphis, where he earned another bachelor's degree. Kenner specializes in advertising, corporate, stock, editorial, and fine art photography, and has participated in numerous photo expeditions to Thailand, Alaska, Brazil, New Zealand, Kenya, Tanzania, and all over the United States and Europe.

CAROL KITMAN worked as staff psychologist for five years at the Smithers Alcoholism Rehabilitation Unit of St. Luke's/Roosevelt Hospital in New York City. She still considers herself an observer but in another mode: Her psychological training has made insightful portraits a specialty, and she has worked for many hospitals and health care services. A native of New York City, Kitman received a bachelor of arts degree from Brooklyn College and a master's degree from City College of New York. She has lived in New Jersey for 36 years. Kitman's work has

appeared recently in *Delta Sky, Mature Outlook, Odyssey,* and *Travel & Leisure*.

SUSIE LEAVINES is a native of New Orleans who has photographed every aspect of New Orleans life. Specializing in scenics, tourism, conventions, and trade shows, she has photographed four U.S. presidents as well as numerous celebrities, politicians, CEOs, and musicians. Leavines' work has been shown in major photography exhibitions in New Orleans and Jackson, Mississippi, as well as appearing in numerous magazines and publications worldwide. She is currently working on photography projects for *Montana Magazine*.

JERRY LeBLOND, a resident of Biddeford, Maine, holds degrees in photography from BSME/Lowell Technical Institute, Nikon School of Photography, and Professional Photographers of America. Employed by Photiques, Ltd., he specializes in architecture, lifestyles, resorts, and sports photography. An avid skier, LeBlond has traveled to Chile and Argentina on assignment for national ski magazines. His work has also been featured in *Geographic Traveler, Newsweek, Travel & Leisure,* and numerous other national magazines, as well as in exhibits sponsored by Kodak and Fuji.

KERRI McCAFFETY, originally from Houston, has lived in New Orleans for more than 10 years. While earning a degree in anthropology at Tulane, she concentrated on ethnographic documentary and went on to photograph people and their environments in Europe, central Africa, and Haiti. Her fine art photography was awarded a prize by William Fagaly, the curator of contemporary art at the New Orleans Museum of Art. McCaffety's work has appeared in *Allure, House and Garden,* and the *Times-Picayune*.

DAVID RAE MORRIS is a freelance photographer for Impact Visuals, New York, who specializes in photojournalism and documentary photography. He holds degrees from the University of Minnesota and Hampshire College in Amherst, Massachusetts. Morris' award-winning photographs have been published in such national magazines as *Time, Newsweek, Parade,* and the *Economist,* as well as in such regional publications, *Southern Exposure, Living Blues,* and *Blues Life.*

ERWIN C. "BUD" NIELSEN, from Tucson, is owner of Images International, a photography firm that handles stock and commercial assignments. He specializes in photographing national and international destinations showing wildlife and other natural and man-made features. Nielsen has also worked with such clients as Barbara Walters of ABC's *20/20* and *National Geographic,* as well as regularly contributing to *RangeFinder* magazine.

RICHARD PASLEY is a Cambridge, Massachusetts-based location photographer who makes annual sojourns to New Orleans, the city he finds most exciting in America. Pasley travels the world shooting a wide range of corporate, industrial, and magazine photography for the likes of AT&T, Fidelity Investments, and *Rolling Stone* magazine. He has photographed some of the biggest events in music history, including the Rock and Roll Hall of Fame induction ceremonies, the first Farm-Aid concert, and Amnesty International concerts.

JONATHAN POSTAL, born in New York City, lived and worked in London, Sydney, Milan, and New Orleans before settling in Memphis. The creative director of *Eye* magazine, his work has been featured in *Rolling Stone, Vanity Fair,* and numerous other magazines. Among his many life experiences, Postal's favorite is the time he was trapped in a 20-foot cage with a 15-foot alligator for 30 minutes.

RAYMOND PUMILIA has been a photographer since he was 14 years old. As an artist, Pumilia works with photographic processes, metal, and

▲ PHILIP GOULD

mixed media. As a commercial photographer, he works for the advertising, music, and fashion industries.

SCOTT SALTZMAN, who moved to New Orleans in 1993, is originally from California and has spent the past several years traveling extensively throughout Europe and the Middle East. He found himself in Slovenia just prior to the Croatian invasion, an experience that greatly affected him. Saltzman is currently self-employed at Ess Pee Designs, where he specializes in all areas of digital photography. His previous clients include Coca-Cola, Harrah's Casino, the *Boston Globe,* and the *Times-Picayune.*

MICHAEL P. SMITH is a native of New Orleans and a graduate of Tulane. He specializes in editorial and documentary photography, with an additional interest in traditional cultures and music. Smith's work has appeared in numerous national publications, including *National Geographic, Time,* and *Newsweek.* His images have also been displayed in the Metropolitan Museum of Art in New York, the Bibliothèque Nationale in Paris, and in the Historic New Orleans Collection.

PAUL TAYLOR has lived in New Orleans since 1981 where he specializes in architectural, interior, editorial, and historic photography. In June 1996 his work was featured on the cover of *New Orleans Magazine.* He is producer and narrator of "A Louisiana Legacy: Historic Properties and the Colonial Dames," a historical documentary. Additionally, Taylor's work has been featured in numerous national magazines, including *Historic Preservation* and *Interiors.*

CAROLYN THORNTON is a freelance photographer and writer from Hattiesburg, Mississippi. Her specialties include travel photography, specifically in the South, and images of steam trains. Thornton has many fond memories of spending childhood summers in New Orleans. Her work has appeared in a variety of national publications, such as the *New York Times, Modern Bride,* the *London Free Press,* and the *Times-Picayune.*

The following photographers also contributed to *New Orleans: Rollin' on the River*: Clint Baker and Brad Crooks.

Index of Profiles